2017 SQA Past Papers with Answers

Advanced Higher
BIOLOGY

2015 Specimen Question Paper,
2016 & 2017 Exams

HODDER GIBSON
AN HACHETTE UK COMPANY

This book contains the official 2015 SQA Specimen Question Paper and the 2016 and 2017 Exams for Advanced Higher Biology, with associated SQA-approved answers modified from the official marking instructions that accompany the paper.

In addition the book contains study skills advice. This advice has been specially commissioned by Hodder Gibson, and has been written by experienced senior teachers and examiners in line with the Advanced Higher syllabus and assessment outlines. This is not SQA material but has been devised to provide further guidance for Advanced Higher examinations.

Hodder Gibson is grateful to the copyright holders, as credited on the final page of the Answer section, for permission to use their material. Every effort has been made to trace the copyright holders and to obtain their permission for the use of copyright material. Hodder Gibson will be happy to receive information allowing us to rectify any error or omission in future editions.

Hachette UK's policy is to use papers that are natural, renewable and recyclable products and made from wood grown in sustainable forests. The logging and manufacturing processes are expected to conform to the environmental regulations of the country of origin.

Orders: please contact Bookpoint Ltd, 130 Park Drive, Milton Park, Abingdon, Oxon OX14 4SE. Telephone: (44) 01235 827720. Fax: (44) 01235 400454. Lines are open 9.00–5.00, Monday to Saturday, with a 24-hour message answering service. Visit our website at www.hoddereducation.co.uk. Hodder Gibson can be contacted direct on: Tel: 0141 333 4650; Fax: 0141 404 8188; email: hoddergibson@hodder.co.uk

This collection first published in 2017 by
Hodder Gibson, an imprint of Hodder Education,
An Hachette UK Company
211 St Vincent Street
Glasgow G2 5QY

Advanced Higher Specimen Question Paper and Answers; Advanced Higher 2016 and 2017 Exam Papers and Answers © Scottish Qualifications Authority. Study Skills section © Hodder Gibson. All rights reserved. Apart from any use permitted under UK copyright law, no part of this publication may be reproduced or transmitted in any form or by any means, electronic or mechanical, including photocopying and recording, or held within any information storage and retrieval system, without permission in writing from the publisher or under licence from the Copyright Licensing Agency Limited. Further details of such licences (for reprographic reproduction) may be obtained from the Copyright Licensing Agency Limited, www.cla.co.uk.

Typeset by Aptara, Inc.

Printed in the UK

A catalogue record for this title is available from the British Library

ISBN: 978-1-5104-2130-1

2 1

2018 2017

Introduction

Study Skills – what you need to know to pass exams!

Pause for thought

Many students might skip quickly through a page like this. After all, we all know how to revise. Do you really though?

Think about this:

"IF YOU ALWAYS DO WHAT YOU ALWAYS DO, YOU WILL ALWAYS GET WHAT YOU HAVE ALWAYS GOT."

Do you like the grades you get? Do you want to do better? If you get full marks in your assessment, then that's great! Change nothing! This section is just to help you get that little bit better than you already are.

There are two main parts to the advice on offer here. The first part highlights fairly obvious things but which are also very important. The second part makes suggestions about revision that you might not have thought about but which WILL help you.

Part 1

DOH! It's so obvious but …

Start revising in good time

Don't leave it until the last minute – this will make you panic.

Make a revision timetable that sets out work time AND play time.

Sleep and eat!

Obvious really, and very helpful. Avoid arguments or stressful things too – even games that wind you up. You need to be fit, awake and focused!

Know your place!

Make sure you know exactly **WHEN and WHERE** your exams are.

Know your enemy!

Make sure you know what to expect in the exam.

How is the paper structured?

How much time is there for each question?

What types of question are involved?

Which topics seem to come up time and time again?

Which topics are your strongest and which are your weakest?

Are all topics compulsory or are there choices?

Learn by DOING!

There is no substitute for past papers and practice papers – they are simply essential! Tackling this collection of papers and answers is exactly the right thing to be doing as your exams approach.

Part 2

People learn in different ways. Some like low light, some bright. Some like early morning, some like evening or night. Some prefer warm, some prefer cold. But everyone uses their BRAIN and the brain works when it is active. Passive learning – sitting gazing at notes – is the most INEFFICIENT way to learn anything. Below you will find tips and ideas for making your revision more effective and maybe even more enjoyable. What follows gets your brain active, and active learning works!

Activity 1 – Stop and review

Step 1

When you have done no more than 5 minutes of revision reading STOP!

Step 2

Write a heading in your own words which sums up the topic you have been revising.

Step 3

Write a summary of what you have revised in no more than two sentences. Don't fool yourself by saying, "I know it, but I cannot put it into words". That just means you don't know it well enough. If you cannot write your summary, revise that section again, knowing that you must write a summary at the end of it. Many of you will have notebooks full of blue/black ink writing. Many of the pages will not be especially attractive or memorable so try to liven them up a bit with colour as you are reviewing and rewriting. **This is a great memory aid, and memory is the most important thing.**

Activity 2 – Use technology!

Why should everything be written down? Have you thought about "mental" maps, diagrams, cartoons and colour to help you learn? And rather than write down notes, why not record your revision material?

What about having a text message revision session with friends? Keep in touch with them to find out how and what they are revising and share ideas and questions.

Why not make a video diary where you tell the camera what you are doing, what you think you have learned and what you still have to do? No one has to see or hear it, but the process of having to organise your thoughts in a formal way to explain something is a very important learning practice.

Be sure to make use of electronic files. You could begin to summarise your class notes. Your typing might be slow, but it will get faster and the typed notes will be easier to read than the scribbles in your class notes. Try to add different fonts and colours to make your work stand out. You can easily Google relevant pictures, cartoons and diagrams which you can copy and paste to make your work more attractive and **MEMORABLE**.

Activity 3 – This is it. Do this and you will know lots!

Step 1

In this task you must be very honest with yourself! Find the SQA syllabus for your subject (www.sqa.org.uk). Look at how it is broken down into main topics called MANDATORY knowledge. That means stuff you MUST know.

Step 2

BEFORE you do ANY revision on this topic, write a list of everything that you already know about the subject. It might be quite a long list but you only need to write it once. It shows you all the information that is already in your long-term memory so you know what parts you do not need to revise!

Step 3

Pick a chapter or section from your book or revision notes. Choose a fairly large section or a whole chapter to get the most out of this activity.

With a buddy, use Skype, Facetime, Twitter or any other communication you have, to play the game "If this is the answer, what is the question?". For example, if you are revising Geography and the answer you provide is "meander", your buddy would have to make up a question like "What is the word that describes a feature of a river where it flows slowly and bends often from side to side?".

Make up 10 "answers" based on the content of the chapter or section you are using. Give this to your buddy to solve while you solve theirs.

Step 4

Construct a wordsearch of at least 10 × 10 squares. You can make it as big as you like but keep it realistic. Work together with a group of friends. Many apps allow you to make wordsearch puzzles online. The words and phrases can go in any direction and phrases can be split. Your puzzle must only contain facts linked to the topic you are revising. Your task is to find 10 bits of information to hide in your puzzle, but you must not repeat information that you used in Step 3. DO NOT show where the words are. Fill up empty squares with random letters. Remember to keep a note of where your answers are hidden but do not show your friends. When you have a complete puzzle, exchange it with a friend to solve each other's puzzle.

Step 5

Now make up 10 questions (not "answers" this time) based on the same chapter used in the previous two tasks. Again, you must find NEW information that you have not yet used. Now it's getting hard to find that new information! Again, give your questions to a friend to answer.

Step 6

As you have been doing the puzzles, your brain has been actively searching for new information. Now write a NEW LIST that contains only the new information you have discovered when doing the puzzles. Your new list is the one to look at repeatedly for short bursts over the next few days. Try to remember more and more of it without looking at it. After a few days, you should be able to add words from your second list to your first list as you increase the information in your long-term memory.

FINALLY! Be inspired...

Make a list of different revision ideas and beside each one write **THINGS I HAVE** tried, **THINGS I WILL** try and **THINGS I MIGHT** try. Don't be scared of trying something new.

And remember – "FAIL TO PREPARE AND PREPARE TO FAIL!"

Advanced Higher Biology

The practice papers in this book give an overall and comprehensive coverage of assessment of **Knowledge** and skills of **Scientific Inquiry** for Advanced Higher Biology.

We recommend that you download and print a copy of the Advanced Higher Biology Course Assessment Specification (CAS) pages 8–17 from the SQA website at www.sqa.org.uk.

The Course

The Advanced Higher Biology Course consists of three National Units. These are Cells and Proteins, Organisms and Evolution, and Investigative Biology. In each of the Units you will be assessed on your ability to demonstrate and apply knowledge of Biology and to demonstrate and apply skills of scientific inquiry.

You must also complete a project, the purpose of which is to allow you to carry out an in-depth investigation of a Biology topic and produce a project–report. You will also take a Course examination.

How the Course is graded

To achieve a Course award for Advanced Higher Biology you must pass all three National Unit Assessments which will be assessed by your school or college on a pass or fail basis. The grade you get depends on the following two Course assessments, which are set and graded by SQA.

1. The project is worth 25% of the grade and is marked out of 30 marks. The majority of the marks will be awarded for applying scientific inquiry skills. The other marks will be awarded for applying related knowledge and understanding.

2. A written Course examination is worth the remaining 75% of the grade. The examination is marked out of 90 marks, 60–70 of which are for the demonstration and application of knowledge with the balance for skills of scientific inquiry.

This book should help you practise the examination part! To pass Advanced Higher Biology with a C grade you will need about 50% of the 120 marks available for the project and the Course examination combined. For a B you will need roughly 60% and, for an A, roughly 70% of the marks available.

The Course examination

The Course examination is a single question paper divided into two sections.

- The first section is an objective test with 25 multiple choice items worth 25 marks.

- The second section is a mix of restricted and extended response questions worth between 1 and 9 marks each for a total of 65 marks. The majority of the marks test knowledge, with an emphasis on the application of knowledge. The remainder test the application of scientific inquiry, analysis and problem solving skills. The first question is usually an extensive data question and there are two extended response questions, one for about 4–5 marks and the other for about 8–10 marks – the longer extended response question will normally have a choice and is usually the last question in the paper.

Altogether, there are 90 marks and you will have 2 hours and 30 minutes to complete the paper. The majority of the marks will be straightforward and linked to grade C but some questions are more demanding and are linked to grade A.

General hints and tips

You should have a copy of the Course Assessment Specification (CAS) for Advanced Higher Biology (you can download it from the SQA website). It is worth spending some time looking at this document, as it indicates what you can be tested on in your examination.

This book contains three practice Advanced Higher Biology examination papers. One is the SQA specimen paper and there are two past exam papers. Notice how similar it is in the way in which it is laid out and the types of question it asks – your own Course examination is going to be very similar as well, so the value of this paper is obvious! Each paper can be attempted in its entirety, or groups of questions on a particular topic or skill area can be attempted. If you are trying a whole examination paper from this book, give yourself a maximum of 2 hours and 30 minutes to complete it. The questions in each paper are laid out roughly in Unit order. Make sure that you spend time in using the answer section to mark your own work – it is especially useful if you can get someone to help you with this.

The marking instructions give acceptable answers with alternatives. You could even grade your work on an A–D basis. The following hints and tips are related to examination techniques as well as avoiding common mistakes. Remember that if you hit problems with a question, you should ask your teacher for help.

Section 1

25 multiple-choice items **25 marks**

- Answer on a grid.
- Do not spend more than 30 minutes on this section.
- Some individual questions might take longer to answer than others – this is quite normal and make sure you use scrap paper if a calculation or any working is needed.
- Some questions can be answered instantly – again, this is normal.
- Do not leave blanks – complete the grid for each question as you work through.
- Try to answer each question in your head without looking at the options. If your answer is there you are home and dry!
- If you are not certain, it is sometimes best to choose the answer that seemed most attractive on first reading the answer options.
- If you are guessing, try to eliminate options before making your guess. If you can eliminate three, you will be left with the correct answer even if you do not recognise it!

Section 2

Restricted and extended response **65 marks**

- Spend about 2 hours on this section.
- A clue to your answer length is the mark allocation – questions restricted to 1 mark can be quite short. If there are 2–3 marks available, your answer will need to be extended and may well have two, three or even four parts.
- The questions are usually laid out in Unit sequence but remember that some questions are designed to cover more than one Unit.
- The C-type questions usually start with "State", "Identify", "Give" or "Name" and often need only a single sentence in response. They will usually be for 1 mark each.
- Questions that begin with "Explain", "Suggest" and "Describe" are usually A-type questions and are likely to have more than one part to the full answer. You will usually have to write a sentence or two and there may be 2 or even 3 marks available.
- Make sure you read over the question twice **before** trying to answer – there will be very important information within the question and underlining or highlighting key words is good technique.
- Using abbreviations like DNA and ATP is fine. The Advanced Higher Biology Course Assessment Specification (CAS) will give you the acceptable abbreviations.

- Don't worry if the questions are in unfamiliar contexts, that's the idea! Just keep calm and read the questions carefully.
- In the large data question (Q1), it is good technique to read the whole stem and then skim the data groups before starting to answer any of the parts.
- In the large data question (Q1), be aware that the first piece of data presented should give the main theme of the question.
- In experimental questions, you must be aware of the different classes of variables, why controls are needed and how reliability and validity might be improved. It is worth spending time on these ideas – they are essential and will come up year after year.
- Note that information which is additional to the main stem may be given within a question part – if it's there, you will need it!
- If instructions in the question ask you to refer to specific groups of data, follow these and don't go beyond them.
- Remember that a conclusion can be seen from data, whereas an explanation will usually require you to supply some background knowledge as well.
- Note that in your answer, you may be asked to "use data to…" – it is essential that you do this.
- Remember to "use values from the graph" when describing graphical information in words, if you are asked to do so.
- Look out for graphs with two Y-axes – these need extra special concentration and anyone can make a mistake!
- In numerical answers, it's good technique to show working and supply units.
- Answers to calculations will not usually have more than two decimal places.
- You should round any numerical answers as appropriate, but two decimal places should be acceptable.
- Ensure that you take error bars into account when evaluating the effects of treatments.
- Do not leave blanks. Always have a go, using the language in the question if you can.

Good luck!

Remember that the rewards for passing Advanced Higher Biology are well worth it! Your pass will help you get the future you want for yourself. In the exam, be confident in your own ability. If you're not sure how to answer a question, trust your instincts and just give it a go anyway.

Keep calm and don't panic! GOOD LUCK!

ADVANCED HIGHER

2015 Specimen Question Paper

National
Qualifications
SPECIMEN ONLY

SQ02/AH/02

Biology
Section 1—Questions

Date — Not applicable

Duration — 2 hours 30 minutes

Instructions for the completion of Section 1 are given on *Page two* of your question and answer booklet SQ02/AH/01.

Record your answers on the answer grid on *Page three* of your question and answer booklet.

Before leaving the examination room you must give your question and answer booklet to the Invigilator; if you do not, you may lose all the marks for this paper.

SECTION 1 — 25 marks

Attempt ALL questions

1. Which of the following is a covalent bond that stabilises the tertiary structure of a protein?

   A   Disulphide bridge

   B   Hydrogen bond

   C   Ionic bond

   D   Hydrophobic interactions

2. A hydrophobic amino acid has an R group that is

   A   negatively charged

   B   positively charged

   C   not polar

   D   polar.

3. A buffered solution of four amino acids was applied to the midline of a strip of electrophoresis gel. The result of running the gel is shown below.

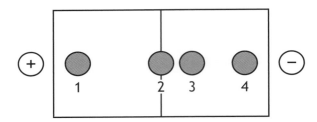

   Which of the amino acids was at its isoelectric point?

   A   1

   B   2

   C   3

   D   4

4. The table shows the number of amino acids in a particular protein and the charge of each amino acid at a certain pH.

Amino acid	Charge	Number
arginine	positive	13
aspartate	negative	9
cysteine	negative	2
histidine	positive	2
glutamate	negative	20
lysine	positive	19
tyrosine	negative	7

Assuming that each amino acid carries a single positive or negative charge, what is the protein's net charge at this pH?

 A   −4

B   −38

C   +4

D   +38

5. The diagram below shows how phosphate is used to modify the conformation of an enzyme, phosphorylase, and so change its activity.

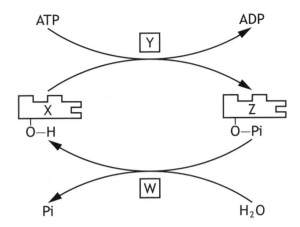

Which line in the table correctly identifies the labels?

	Kinase	Phosphatase	Phosphorylase
A	Y	Z	W
B	W	Y	Z
C	X	Y	W
D	Y	W	Z

6. The diagram below shows the distribution of protein molecules in a cell membrane.

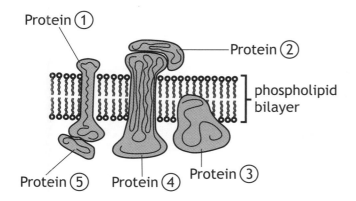

Which line in the table correctly identifies a peripheral and an integral membrane protein?

	Peripheral membrane protein	Integral membrane protein
A	1	5
B	2	1
C	3	4
D	5	2

7. The sodium-potassium pump spans the plasma membrane. Various processes involved in the active transport of sodium and potassium ions take place either inside the cell (intracellular) or outside the cell (extracellular).

Which line in the table correctly applies to the binding of potassium ions?

	Binding location of potassium ions	Conformation of transport protein
A	extracellular	not phosphorylated
B	intracellular	not phosphorylated
C	extracellular	phosphorylated
D	intracellular	phosphorylated

8. The diagram below shows a haemocytometer grid that was used to estimate the number of cells in a 10 cm³ microbial culture. The depth of the counting chamber is 0·2 mm.

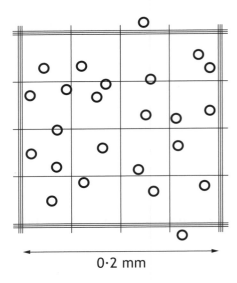

0·2 mm

The number of cells in the 10 cm³ culture was

A   2·75 × 10⁷

B   2·5 × 10⁷

C   2·25 × 10⁷

D   1·6 × 10³.

9. The contribution of aquaporins (AQPs) to osmosis was studied by measuring the rate of movement of radioactive water across a plasma membrane. Rates were measured in either isotonic or hypertonic external solution when the pores were either open or closed. Results are shown in the table.

External solution	Rate of water movement (units s⁻¹)	
	Open AQPs	Closed AQPs
Isotonic	2·5	1·0
Hypertonic	20·0	1·8

Which of the following is the dependent variable in the experiment?

A   External solution

B   Radioactivity of water

C   Rate of water movement

D   Aquaporins

10. To which group of signalling molecules do steroid hormones belong?

    A   Extracellular hydrophobic

    B   Extracellular hydrophilic

    C   Peptide hormones

    D   Neurotransmitters

11. The following diagrams represent stages in an indirect ELISA used to detect the presence of a poisonous toxin in food samples. The test shown is positive. Identify the diagram that represents the correct sequence of events in the ELISA.

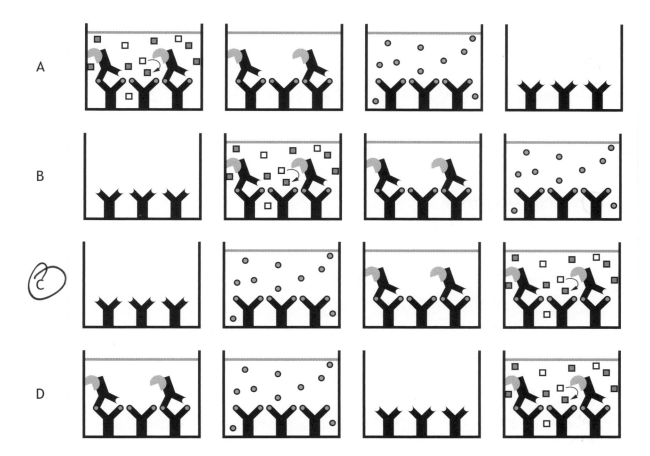

12. Identify which of the following proteins are involved in apoptosis.

    1   Caspases

    2   p53

    3   DNAses

    A   2 only

    B   1 and 2 only

    C   1 and 3 only

    D   1, 2 and 3

13. Animal cells growing in culture are found to spend 20% of their time in the G2 phase of the cell cycle. G2 lasts for 4 hours.

    If cells spend 12% of their time in the M phase, how long does this last?

    A   2 hours 4 minutes

    B   2 hours 12 minutes

    (C)   2 hours 24 minutes

    D   2 hours 40 minutes

14. Name the ion which is pumped across membranes by bacteriorhodopsin.

    A   Sodium

    B   Potassium

    (C)   Chloride

    D   Hydrogen

15. Which of the following would be true if a population's gene pool remained unaltered for many generations?

    (A)   Mating was random

    B   Migration was common

    C   Genetic drift had occurred

    D   Certain alleles had a selective advantage

16. Identify the line in the table that applies to r-selected species.

	many offspring produced	prolonged parental care
A	yes	yes
B	yes	no
C	no	yes
D	no	no

17. *C. elegans* is a model organism of the phylum

    A   Chordata

    B   Arthropoda

    (C)   Nematoda

    D   Mollusca.

18. From the following list, identify all the possible sources of DNA during horizontal gene transfer.

    1　viruses

    2　plasmids

    3　bacterial cells

    4　gametes

    A　1 and 2 only

    B　2 and 3 only

    C　1, 2 and 3 only

    D　1, 2 ,3 and 4

19. The following diagram is **drawn to scale** and indicates the position of four linked genes on a chromosome.

    W　　　　　　　X　　　　　　　　　　　　Y　　　　　Z

    Identify the column in the table that gives the correct recombination frequencies for the genes in the chromosome map shown above.

Genes	Recombination frequency (%)			
	A	B	C	D
X and Z	17	19	17	15
W and Z	25	25	23	23
Y and W	19	17	15	17
Z and Y	6	8	8	6
X and W	8	6	6	8

20. The error bars on the graphs represent standard errors in the mean (SEM). Which graph shows significantly different reliable data?

A

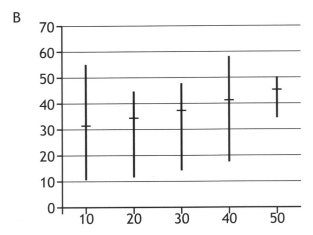

B

C

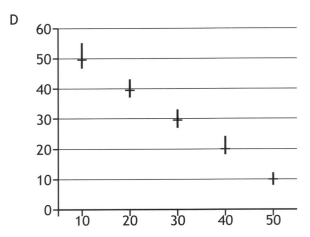

D

21. *Anolis* lizards are found on Caribbean islands. They feed on prey of various sizes.

Histogram 1 shows the range of prey length eaten by *Anolis marmoratus* on the island of Jarabacoa, where there are five other *Anolis* species.

Histogram 2 shows the range of prey length eaten by *Anolis marmoratus* on the island of Marie Galante, where it is the only *Anolis* species.

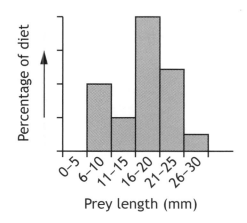

Histogram 1: Jarabacoa

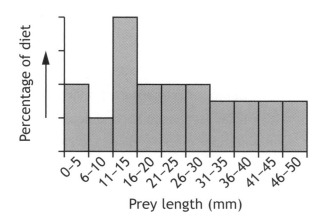

Histogram 2: Marie Galante Island

Which of the following statements could explain the different range of prey sizes eaten by *Anolis marmoratus* on the two islands?

A   Larger numbers of prey are found on Marie Galante.

B   *Anolis marmoratus* occupies its fundamental niche on Jarabacoa.

C   *Anolis marmoratus* occupies its realised niche on Marie Galante.

D   Resource partitioning takes place on Jarabacoa.

22. Herd immunity threshold is

A   The density of hosts in a population required to prevent an epidemic

B   The density of resistant hosts in a population required to prevent an epidemic

C   The density of hosts in a population required for transmission to cause an epidemic

D   The density of parasites in a population required to cause an epidemic.

23. Reverse transcriptase catalyses the production of

A   DNA from RNA

B   DNA from DNA

C   mRNA from DNA

D   tRNA from mRNA.

24. Which of the following would **not** provide long-term control of parasites following a natural disaster?

A   Immunisation

B   Improved sanitation

C   Co-ordinated vector control

D   Drug treatment of infected humans

25. The formula N = MC/R is used to estimate population size using mark and recapture data.

> N = population estimate
>
> M = number first captured, marked and released
>
> C = total number in second capture
>
> R = number marked in second capture

In a survey to estimate a woodlouse population, the following data were obtained:

> Woodlice captured, marked and released   = 80
>
> Marked woodlice in second capture   = 24
>
> Unmarked woodlice in second capture   = 96

The estimated population of the woodlice was

A   200

B   320

C   400

D   3840.

**[END OF SECTION 1. NOW ATTEMPT THE QUESTIONS IN SECTION 2
OF YOUR QUESTION AND ANSWER BOOKLET]**

FOR OFFICIAL USE

AH

National Qualifications
SPECIMEN ONLY

Mark

SQ02/AH/01

Biology
Section 1 — Answer Grid and Section 2

Date — Not applicable

Duration — 2 hours 30 minutes

Fill in these boxes and read what is printed below.

Full name of centre

Town

Forename(s)

Surname

Number of seat

Date of birth

Day	Month	Year	Scottish candidate number

Total marks — 90

SECTION 1 — 25 marks

Attempt ALL questions.

Instructions for completion of Section 1 are given on *Page two*.

SECTION 2 — 65 marks

Attempt ALL questions.

Write your answers clearly in the spaces provided in this booklet. Additional space for answers and rough work is provided at the end of this booklet. If you use this space you must clearly identify the question number you are attempting. Any rough work must be written in this booklet. You should score through your rough work when you have written your final copy.

Use **blue** or **black** ink.

Before leaving the examination room you must give this booklet to the Invigilator; if you do not you may lose all the marks for this paper.

SQA ©

MARKS | DO NOT WRITE IN THIS MARGIN

5.   **(continued)**

(c)   (i)   Explain how the data support the conclusion that the thyroid gland has large stores of thyroxine.

1

_____

_____

(ii)   Explain why the changes in metabolic rate have been presented as percentages.

1

_____

_____

MARKS | DO NOT WRITE IN THIS MARGIN

6. Rod cells and cone cells are photoreceptors in vertebrate eyes. Membranes in these cells contain rhodopsin, a protein molecule that has a light-absorbing component. Rhodopsin generates a nerve impulse when light is absorbed.

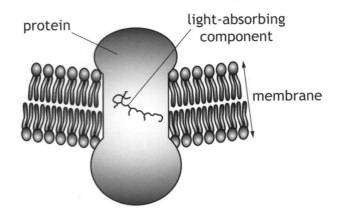

(a) Name the light-absorbing component of rhodopsin.

1

(b) Explain the mechanism by which the absorption of a photon by rhodopsin leads to the generation of a nerve impulse.

2

(c) Give one feature of the photoreceptor system in rods that allows these cells to function in low light intensity.

1

MARKS | DO NOT WRITE IN THIS MARGIN

7. A type of haemophilia results when a gene that codes for a blood clotting factor, factor VIII, is mutated. This gene is located on the X chromosome. Mutated alleles do not produce functional factor VIII.

    (a) Explain why men are more likely than women to be affected by this type of haemophilia.

    2

    _____

    _____

    _____

    (b) An unaffected man and a carrier woman have a daughter and a son.

    State the probability of each child being able to produce functional factor VIII.

    2

    Space for calculation and working

    Daughter _____

    Son   _____

    (c) (i) Explain the importance of inactivation of the X chromosome in females.

    1

    _____

    _____

        (ii) Analysis of a female carrier showed that her blood contained only 42% of the normal levels of functional factor VIII.

        Suggest why this value was lower than predicted.

    1

    _____

    _____

MARKS | DO NOT WRITE IN THIS MARGIN

8. Describe how the events that occur during crossing over contribute to the production of variable gametes.

4

_____

_____

_____

_____

_____

_____

9. The following figure shows the life cycle of the macroparasitic flatworm called *Schistosoma japonicum*. The flatworm can live for many years within a host. In humans, if untreated, it causes the disease schistosomiasis (bilharzia) that can be fatal.

Life cycle of *Schistosoma japonicum*

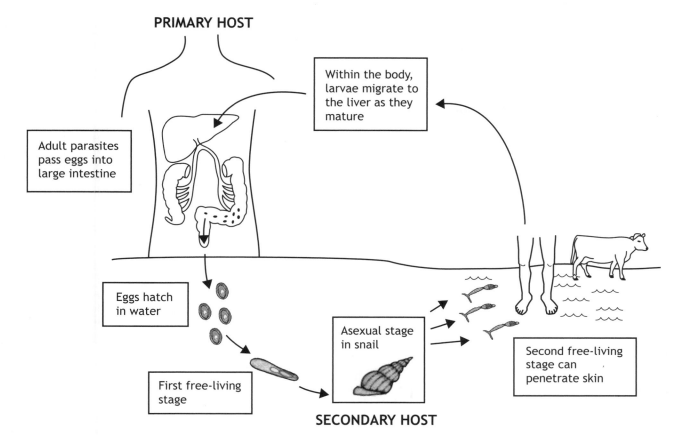

(a)   (i)   Explain why the snail may **not** be described as a vector.

MARKS 1

_____

_____

(ii) Suggest a feature of this parasite's life cycle that can lead to an increased rate of transmission.

1

_____

_____

MARKS | DO NOT WRITE IN THIS MARGIN

9. (continued)

(b) Parasites living inside a host will be exposed to attack by the host's immune system.

Describe one way in which parasites may overcome the immune response of their hosts.

1

_____

_____

(c) Describe the Red Queen hypothesis.

2

_____

_____

MARKS | DO NOT WRITE IN THIS MARGIN

10. Fur seals spend most of their lives feeding in Antarctic seas. During the short summer they come ashore to breed.

The figure below shows the number of fur seals breeding on Signy Island from 1956 to 1986.

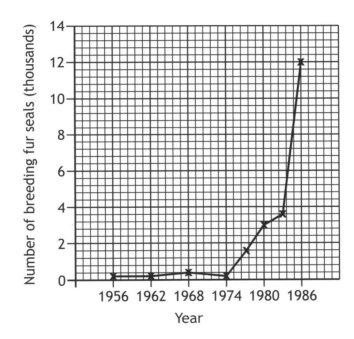

(a) Calculate the percentage increase in the size of the breeding seal population between 1980 and 1986.

Space for calculation and working

_____ %

1

MARKS | DO NOT WRITE IN THIS MARGIN

10. **(continued)**

(b) Permanent quadrats were established to investigate the effect of fur seals on ground cover plants. The table shows the mean percentage of cover of a number of plant species sampled in the permanent quadrats in 1965 and 1985.

Plant species	Percentage cover (%)	
	1965	1985
Drepanocladus uncinatus	30	0
Bryum algens	49	0
Tortula filaris	16	0
Tortula saxicola	4	4
Prasiola crispa	1	41

(i) Explain the changes in percentage cover between 1965 and 1985. **2**

_____

_____

_____

(ii) Suggest why the percentage cover in 1985 is not 100%. **1**

_____

_____

(c) (i) Describe one consideration that must be taken into account when carrying out sampling in an ecosystem. **1**

_____

_____

(ii) Describe the process of stratified sampling. **1**

_____

_____

MARKS | DO NOT WRITE IN THIS MARGIN

11. Answer **either A or B** in the space below.

A Describe the specific cellular defences that protect mammals from parasite infection.   8

OR

B Describe courtship behaviours that affect reproductive success.   8

[END OF SPECIMEN QUESTION PAPER]

ADDITIONAL SPACE FOR ANSWERS AND ROUGH WORK

MARKS | DO NOT WRITE IN THIS MARGIN

MARKS | DO NOT WRITE IN THIS MARGIN

ADDITIONAL SPACE FOR ANSWERS AND ROUGH WORK

Page twenty-three

[BLANK PAGE]

DO NOT WRITE ON THIS PAGE

ADVANCED HIGHER

2016

National
Qualifications
2016

X707/77/02

Biology
Section 1 — Questions

MONDAY, 9 MAY
9:00 AM – 11:30 AM

Instructions for the completion of Section 1 are given on *Page two* of your question and answer booklet X707/77/01.

Record your answers on the answer grid on *Page three* of your question and answer booklet.

Before leaving the examination room you must give your question and answer booklet to the Invigilator; if you do not, you may lose all the marks for this paper.

18. Ellis-van Creveld syndrome is a rare genetic condition. It is much more common in an isolated population in North America, which was founded by a small number of individuals, than in the general population.

   The most likely explanation for this is

   A   natural selection

   B   sexual selection

   C   random mutation

   D   genetic drift.

19. The frequency of a given allele in a population is a measure of how common that allele is as a proportion of the total number of copies of all alleles at a specific locus. For a locus with one dominant allele (A) and one recessive allele (a), the frequency of the dominant allele (p) and the frequency of the recessive allele (q) can be used to calculate the genetic variation of a population using the equations below.

$$p + q = 1$$

p = frequency of A allele
q = frequency of a allele

$$p^2 + 2pq + q^2 = 1$$

p^2 = frequency of homozygous (AA) individuals
q^2 = frequency of homozygous (aa) individuals
$2pq$ = frequency of heterozygous (Aa) individuals

   If the allele frequency of the recessive allele is 0·7, the proportion of individuals that would be heterozygous is

   A   0·09

   B   0·21

   C   0·42

   D   0·49.

[Turn over

20. In the fruit fly *Drosophila melanogaster* the gene for eye colour is sex-linked. The allele for red eye (R) is dominant to the allele for white eye (r).

A cross between two flies produced the offspring shown in the table below.

Sex of offspring	Number with white eyes	Number with red eyes
female	23	22
male	21	22

The genotypes of the parents in this cross were

A X^rX^r and X^RY

B X^RX^r and X^rY

C X^RX^r and X^RY

D X^RX^R and X^rY.

21. Which row in the table best describes r-selected species?

	Number of offspring	Offspring survival rate	Parental care
A	many	low	little
B	few	high	extensive
C	many	high	extensive
D	few	low	little

22. Shags and cormorants both belong to the genus *Phalacrocorax*. They look very similar and nest near each other on the same cliffs. The table below shows the main components of each bird's diet.

Prey	Percentage composition of diet	
	Shag (Phalacrocorax aristotelis)	Cormorant (Phalacrocorax carbo)
sand eels	33	0
sprats	49	1
flatfish	1	26
shrimps	2	33
gobies	4	17
other fish	4	18

The data in the table show

A   competitive exclusion

B   competition within each species

C   resource partitioning

D   the fundamental niche of each species.

[Turn over

23. A species of parasitic wasp (*Nasonia vitripennis*) lays its eggs in the larvae of flies where the eggs develop. This species displays a behaviour called *"superparasitism"* where, following the laying of eggs by one wasp, a second wasp may superparasitise the same host by also laying its eggs.

Researchers investigated the effects of superparasitism on the brood size and sex ratio of offspring in this species. Results were compared to a control that had been parasitised only once. Researchers were able to distinguish between the offspring of the first and second wasp.

Results are shown in the table below.

Offspring	Degree of parasitism		
	Superparasitism		Single parasitism control
	Wasp 1	Wasp 2	
brood size	18 ± 3	17 ± 4	20 ± 2
percentage of males	7 ± 2	22 ± 4	6 ± 1

The following statements refer to the data in the table.

1   Superparasitism significantly increased the percentage of males produced by both wasp 1 and wasp 2.

2   Superparasitism significantly increased the percentage of males produced by wasp 2 only.

3   Superparasitism had no significant effect on brood size.

4   Superparasitism significantly decreased the brood size produced by wasps 1 and 2.

Which of these statements are valid conclusions supported by the data?

A   1 and 3

B   1 and 4

C   2 and 3

D   2 and 4

24. The statements below describe events that occur following the engulfing of a pathogen by a phagocyte of the mammalian immune system.

   P   long term survival of lymphocytes
   Q   antigen presentation to lymphocytes
   R   antibody production by lymphocytes
   S   clonal selection of B lymphocytes

   The correct sequence in which these events occur is

   A   Q, R, S, P
   B   R, Q, P, S
   C   S, Q, P, R
   D   Q, S, R, P.

25. Florida scrubjays have evolved a co-operative breeding system in which helper birds assist breeding pairs in raising young. The table below compares the effect of helpers on the breeding success of birds that are either experienced or inexperienced breeders.

Breeding experience of breeding pairs	Average number of offspring reared	
	Without helpers	With helpers
inexperienced	1·24	2·20
experienced	1·80	2·38

Helpers increase the average number of offspring reared by inexperienced breeding pairs compared to experienced breeding pairs by

   A   19%
   B   23%
   C   45%
   D   60%.

[END OF SECTION 1. NOW ATTEMPT THE QUESTIONS IN SECTION 2 OF YOUR QUESTION AND ANSWER BOOKLET]

[BLANK PAGE]

DO NOT WRITE ON THIS PAGE

FOR OFFICIAL USE

National Qualifications 2016

Mark

X707/77/01

Biology
Section 1 — Answer Grid
and Section 2

MONDAY, 9 MAY

9:00 AM – 11:30 AM

Fill in these boxes and read what is printed below.

Full name of centre

Town

Forename(s)

Surname

Number of seat

Date of birth

Day	Month	Year	Scottish candidate number

Total marks — 90

SECTION 1 — 25 marks

Attempt ALL questions.

Instructions for completion of Section 1 are given on *Page two*.

SECTION 2 — 65 marks

Attempt ALL questions.

A Supplementary Sheet for Question 1 is enclosed inside the front cover of this question paper. Write your answers clearly in the spaces provided in this booklet. Additional space for answers and rough work is provided at the end of this booklet. If you use this space you must clearly identify the question number you are attempting. Any rough work must be written in this booklet. You should score through your rough work when you have written your final copy.

Use **blue** or **black** ink.

Before leaving the examination room you must give this booklet to the Invigilator; if you do not you may lose all the marks for this paper.

SECTION 1 — 25 marks

The questions for Section 1 are contained in the question paper X707/77/02.

Read these and record your answers on the answer grid on *Page three* opposite.

Use **blue** or **black** ink. Do NOT use gel pens or pencil.

1. The answer to each question is **either** A, B, C or D. Decide what your answer is, then fill in the appropriate bubble (see sample question below).

2. There is **only one correct** answer to each question.

3. Any rough working should be done on the additional space for answers and rough work at the end of this booklet.

Sample Question

The thigh bone is called the

    A   humerus

    B   femur

    C   tibia

    D   fibula.

The correct answer is **B** — femur. The answer **B** bubble has been clearly filled in (see below).

Changing an answer

If you decide to change your answer, cancel your first answer by putting a cross through it (see below) and fill in the answer you want. The answer below has been changed to **D**.

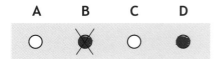

If you then decide to change back to an answer you have already scored out, put a tick (✓) to the **right** of the answer you want, as shown below:

    or

SECTION 1 — Answer Grid

	A	B	C	D
1	○	○	○	○
2	○	○	○	○
3	○	○	○	○
4	○	○	○	○
5	○	○	○	○
6	○	○	○	○
7	○	○	○	○
8	○	○	○	○
9	○	○	○	○
10	○	○	○	○
11	○	○	○	○
12	○	○	○	○
13	○	○	○	○
14	○	○	○	○
15	○	○	○	○
16	○	○	○	○
17	○	○	○	○
18	○	○	○	○
19	○	○	○	○
20	○	○	○	○
21	○	○	○	○
22	○	○	○	○
23	○	○	○	○
24	○	○	○	○
25	○	○	○	○

[Turn over

[BLANK PAGE]

DO NOT WRITE ON THIS PAGE

[Turn over for next question

DO NOT WRITE ON THIS PAGE

MARKS | DO NOT WRITE IN THIS MARGIN

SECTION 2 — 65 marks

Attempt ALL questions

It should be noted that question 11 contains a choice.

1. Read through the Supplementary Sheet for Question 1 before attempting this question.

    (a) **Refer to Figure 2 in the Supplementary Sheet for Question 1.**

        (i) Use the data to describe the egg-laying of uninfected mosquitoes.   **2**

        _____

        _____

        _____

        (ii) If the box plots were perfectly symmetrical, mean values for egg-laying would be very close to median values.

        State what can be deduced about the **mean** number of eggs laid by infected mosquitoes in relation to the median value.   **1**

        _____

        (iii) Describe the effect that *Plasmodium* infection has on the fecundity of mosquitoes used in the study.   **1**

        _____

    (b) **Refer to Figure 3 in the Supplementary Sheet for Question 1.**

        (i) The data shows that infection by *Plasmodium* appears to increase the longevity of female mosquitoes.

        Explain why the difference between the two groups can be regarded as significant.   **1**

        _____

        (ii) Suggest a benefit to the parasite of its vector living longer.   **1**

        _____

        _____

MARKS | DO NOT WRITE IN THIS MARGIN

1. **(continued)**

(c) **Refer to Figure 4 in the Supplementary Sheet for Question 1.**

(i) Explain what the lines of best fit indicate about the relationship between longevity and fecundity in both infected and uninfected mosquitoes.

2

_____

_____

_____

_____

(ii) State, with justification, whether or not this data is reliable.

1

_____

_____

_____

[Turn over

MARKS | DO NOT WRITE IN THIS MARGIN

2. Scientists have reported that neurons produced in cell culture from human stem cells have the potential to function when grafted into the site of a spinal injury in rats.

(a) State why the cell culture medium in which the neurons were cultured should contain serum.

1

_____

(b) Scientists used a haemocytometer to perform a cell count to calculate the number of stem cells that developed into neurons.

The diagram below represents a sample from a culture placed in a haemocytometer and viewed under a microscope.

The grid is **0·1 mm** in depth.

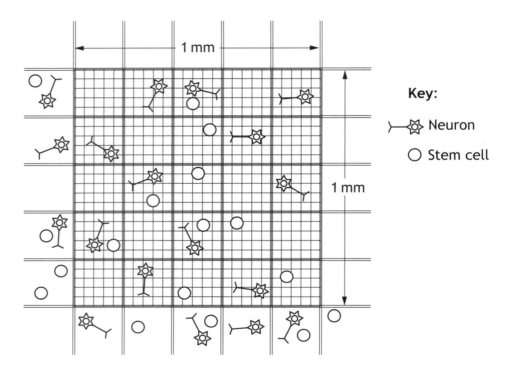

Key:

>─✵ Neuron

○ Stem cell

(i) Calculate the number of **neurons** in 1 cm³ of the culture.

Space for calculation

1

_____ neurons

(ii) Suggest **one** disadvantage of cell counts performed using the haemocytometer.

1

_____

MARKS | DO NOT WRITE IN THIS MARGIN

2.   **(continued)**

(c)   Bright field microscopy was used to view the cells grafted into the site of spinal injury.

State another type of biological material that can be viewed using bright field microscopy.

1

_____

(d)   In studies involving animals, state **one** way in which harm to the animals can be minimised.

1

_____

[Turn over

3. Multiple sclerosis (MS) is a neurological condition in which the body's immune system destroys the myelin sheath that surrounds and insulates nerve axons.

A clinical study was carried out into the effects of a new drug *interferon beta-1b* for this condition. A randomised trial, with a negative control group (placebo), was carried out across four different health centres. During the study patients were given one of three treatments: 0·00 mg (placebo), 0·05 mg or 0·25 mg interferon. The patients administered the drug themselves at home.

The study measured how effective the drug was by asking patients to record any worsening of symptoms after 2 years of treatment. The study involved 372 patients aged 18-50 years. Fourteen patients dropped out before completing the trial.

Patients' results are shown in Table 1.

Table 1

Level of interferon beta-1b in treatment (mg)	Proportion of patients reporting no worsening of symptoms after 2 years of treatment (%)
0·00	16
0·05	18
0·25	25

At one health centre 52 patients were MRI scanned every 6 weeks to monitor any new damage to nerve tissue. The results are shown in Table 2.

Table 2

Level of interferon beta-1b in treatment (mg)	Proportion of patients showing new nerve damage (%)
0·00	29
0·05	no data recorded
0·25	6

(a) Identify the independent variable in this trial. 1

_____

(b) This trial was carried out *in vivo*.

State **one** advantage of this type of trial. 1

_____

_____

MARKS | DO NOT WRITE IN THIS MARGIN

3. **(continued)**

(c) Explain why a placebo group was included in this trial.　1

_____

_____

(d) Suggest **one** way in which the results of the trial may not be reliable.　1

_____

_____

(e) Describe an ethical issue that the researchers would need to consider before this trial.　1

_____

_____

(f) Suggest **two** conclusions that can be drawn from the results of this trial.　2

Conclusion 1 _____

_____

Conclusion 2 _____

_____

[Turn over

MARKS | DO NOT WRITE IN THIS MARGIN

4. Sickle cell anaemia is an inherited blood disorder that reduces the ability of red blood cells to transport oxygen round the body by changing the structure of haemoglobin.

In sickle cell anaemia, the primary structure of a haemoglobin subunit is altered; the amino acid glutamic acid is substituted by the amino acid valine.

The structures of glutamic acid and valine are shown below.

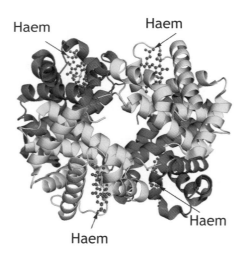

(a) State the class of amino acids to which valine belongs.   1

_____

(b) Identify **one** type of secondary structure shown in the haemoglobin molecule in the figure below.   1

_____

MARKS | DO NOT WRITE IN THIS MARGIN

4. (continued)

(c) Explain the term cooperativity in relation to oxygen binding to haemoglobin.

1

_____

_____

(d) The graph below shows the oxygen saturation of haemoglobin at different oxygen pressures for an individual with normal haemoglobin and for another individual with sickle cell haemoglobin.

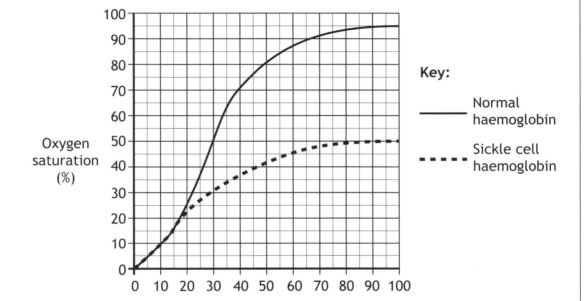

Key:

——— Normal haemoglobin

- - - - Sickle cell haemoglobin

Oxygen saturation (%) — vertical axis

Oxygen pressure (units) — horizontal axis

Use the graph to compare the oxygen saturation of normal and sickle cell haemoglobin as oxygen pressure increases.

2

_____

_____

_____

_____

(e) Molecules of sickle cell haemoglobin clump together preventing access to oxygen binding sites.

Suggest why this is a result of the substitution of glutamic acid by valine.

1

_____

_____

[Turn over

MARKS | DO NOT WRITE IN THIS MARGIN

5. Describe the structure of spindle fibres and explain their role in the movement of chromosomes during cell division.   **4**

_____

_____

_____

_____

_____

_____

_____

MARKS | DO NOT WRITE IN THIS MARGIN

6. The sodium potassium pump (Na/KATPase) is a membrane protein found in animal cells.

(a) Give **one** function of sodium potassium pumps.   **1**

_____

_____

(b) Describe the role of ATP in altering the affinity of the pump for sodium ions (Na^+).   **2**

_____

_____

_____

(c) Digoxin is a chemical that inhibits the sodium potassium pump by binding to the potassium ion (K^+) binding site as shown in the diagram below.

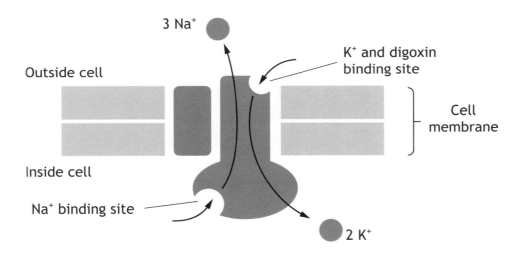

Explain why binding by digoxin prevents further binding of sodium (Na^+) ions by the pump.   **2**

_____

_____

_____

_____

[Turn over

MARKS | DO NOT WRITE IN THIS MARGIN

7. Binding of antidiuretic hormone (ADH) to its receptor on the plasma membrane of kidney collecting duct cells triggers the recruitment of water channel proteins as shown below.

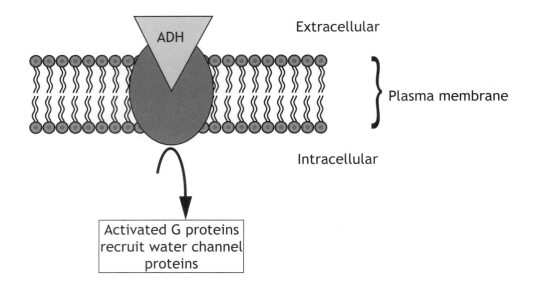

(a) (i) Name the water channel protein involved in this process.   **1**

_____

(ii) Name the process by which a response within the cell is triggered by the binding of ADH to its cell surface receptor.   **1**

_____

MARKS | DO NOT WRITE IN THIS MARGIN

7. **(continued)**

(b) A urine output of greater than 0·05 litres per kg body mass per day is considered diagnostic of diabetes insipidus. The bar chart below shows the urine output over 6 days of a 70 kg individual being investigated for diabetes insipidus. During days 3 and 4 the individual was treated with the drug *desmopressin*, a synthetic form of ADH.

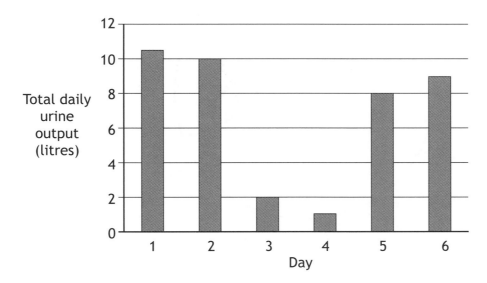

(i)   Use the data to confirm that a diagnosis of diabetes insipidus is correct for this individual.   **1**

Space for calculation

_____

_____

_____

(ii) Give evidence from the graph that supports the conclusion that *desmopressin* is an effective treatment.   **1**

_____

_____

(iii) Diabetes insipidus results from failure to recruit water channel proteins to the cell membrane.

Identify the cause of recruitment failure in this individual.   **1**

_____

[Turn over

MARKS | DO NOT WRITE IN THIS MARGIN

8. The diagram below shows the pairing of homologous chromosomes in a cell undergoing meiosis.

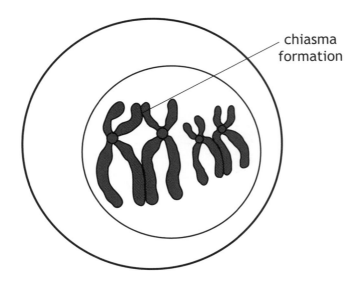

chiasma formation

(a) Name the type of cell that undergoes meiosis.

1

_____

(b) (i) Explain how the chiasma formation between the paired homologous chromosomes shown in the diagram leads to variation.

2

_____

_____

_____

_____

(ii) Name the process that ensures haploid gametes produced by meiosis contain a mixture of chromosomes of maternal and paternal origin.

1

_____

[Turn over for next question

DO NOT WRITE ON THIS PAGE

9. In 1971, biologists moved five adult pairs of Italian wall lizards (*Podarcis sicula*) from their small home island of Kopiste to the neighbouring small island of Mrcaru, which did not have a lizard population. On their return in 2005 Mrcaru was found to have a large population of *P. sicula* (confirmed by genetic analysis) with significantly larger heads and a greater bite force than the lizards from Kopiste. Their digestive systems were also found to contain microorganisms that assist in the breakdown of plant cell walls.

    The summer diets of the two lizard populations are shown below.

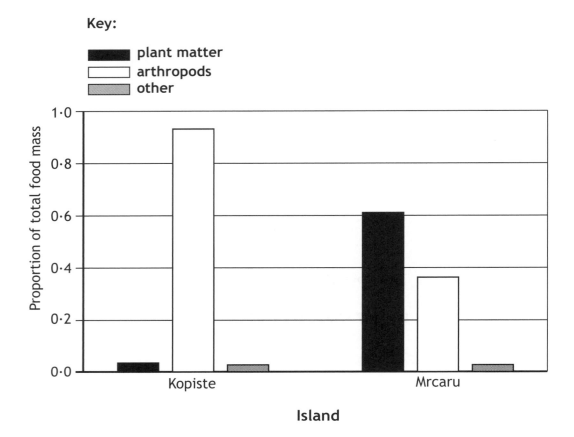

    (a) Describe the most significant change in the summer diet of the lizards on Mrcaru.   1

    _____

    _____

MARKS | DO NOT WRITE IN THIS MARGIN

9. (continued)

(b) (i) Explain how the information supports the conclusion that the changes to the lizard population on Mrcaru were the result of natural selection.

2

_____

_____

_____

_____

(ii) Evolution of the lizards on Mrcaru occurred very rapidly.

State **one** factor that can increase the rate of evolution.

1

_____

(c) This study involved taking representative samples of the lizard populations on the two islands.

State **one** feature of a representative sample.

1

_____

_____

[Turn over

MARKS | DO NOT WRITE IN THIS MARGIN

10. The Figures below show male and female capercaillies (*Tetrao urogallus*) which are found in some Scottish pine forests. Males are much larger and darker than females and the breast feathers of the male have a metallic green sheen.

male capercaillie

female capercaillie

(a) State the term used to indicate the different body forms of males and females belonging to this species.   1

_____

(b) Capercaillies are a lekking species. Males perform displays during which they fan their tails, hold their wings down and make a variety of sounds. These features, which are attractive to females, are thought to serve as honest signals.

(i) Explain what is meant by a lekking species.   1

_____

_____

(ii) Explain why this display is often given as an example of sexual selection.   1

_____

_____

(iii) If the display provides honest signals, state the benefit that may be obtained by females receiving these signals.   1

_____

_____

MARKS | DO NOT WRITE IN THIS MARGIN

10.   (continued)

(c)   Peacocks are the males of another lekking bird species, *Pavo cristatus*, whose natural habitat is the dense forests of South-East Asia. As well as the visual stimulus of a tail-feather display, peacocks, during mating, can emit a distinctive "hoot". These hoots are loud enough to be heard by other females, out of sight of the lek, who may be attracted by the calls and provide the dominant males at the lek with additional mating partners.

   (i)   Suggest why auditory stimuli are advantageous to species inhabiting forest ecosystems.   **1**

   _____

   _____

   (ii)   Recent research has found that some peacocks emit hoots in the complete absence of females at the lek. Females are still attracted to the lek by these sounds. Such "solo" hoots have been described as "dishonest signals".

   Explain what is meant by a "dishonest signal" in this behaviour.   **1**

   _____

   _____

[Turn over for next question

MARKS | DO NOT WRITE IN THIS MARGIN

11.   Answer **either A or B** in the space below and on *Page twenty-five*.

A   Discuss reproduction under the following headings:

(i)   costs and benefits of sexual reproduction;   **4**

(ii)   asexual reproduction as a successful reproductive strategy.   **5**

OR

B   Discuss endoparasitic infections under the following headings:

(i)   difficulties involved in their treatment and control;   **7**

(ii)   benefits of improved parasite control to human populations.   **2**

Labelled diagrams may be used where appropriate.

SPACE FOR ANSWER FOR QUESTION 11

Page twenty-five

[END OF QUESTION PAPER]

ADDITIONAL SPACE FOR ANSWERS AND ROUGH WORK

MARKS | DO NOT WRITE IN THIS MARGIN

ADDITIONAL SPACE FOR ANSWERS AND ROUGH WORK

[BLANK PAGE]

DO NOT WRITE ON THIS PAGE

National
Qualifications
2016

X707/77/11

Biology
Supplementary Sheet

MONDAY, 9 MAY

9:00 AM – 11:30 AM

Supplementary Sheet for Question 1

1. Malaria is caused by unicellular parasites in the genus *Plasmodium*. Figure 1 shows the life cycle of the parasite with respect to its human and mosquito hosts.

Figure 1

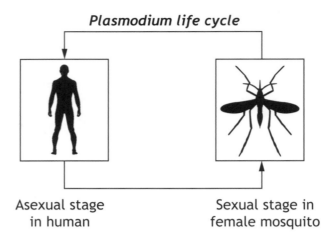

Plasmodium life cycle

Asexual stage
in human

Sexual stage in
female mosquito

Malaria is a well-researched tropical disease of humans, but less is known about the effects of the parasite on its mosquito vector.

The parasite *Plasmodium relictum* causes malaria in birds. A recent study has been carried out to investigate the effects of this parasite on the mosquito *Culex pipiens*. In particular, two aspects were investigated: fecundity (number of eggs laid) and longevity (measured as survival after egg laying) of the mosquitoes.

In Figure 2, box-and-whisker plots show the total egg production by large numbers of uninfected and infected female mosquitoes.

Figure 2

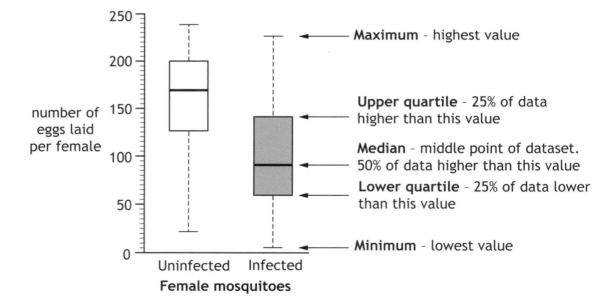

number of eggs laid per female

Maximum – highest value

Upper quartile – 25% of data higher than this value

Median – middle point of dataset. 50% of data higher than this value

Lower quartile – 25% of data lower than this value

Minimum – lowest value

Uninfected   Infected
Female mosquitoes

1. **(continued)**

Figure 3 shows mean survival times after egg laying for uninfected and infected female mosquitoes.

Figure 3

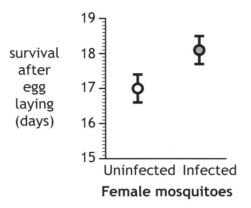

Fecundity and longevity were measured in the same individual female mosquitoes to see if there was a relationship between the two variables.

The lines of best fit for mosquito survival against the number of eggs each female laid were plotted for uninfected females and infected females.

This data is shown in Figure 4.

Figure 4

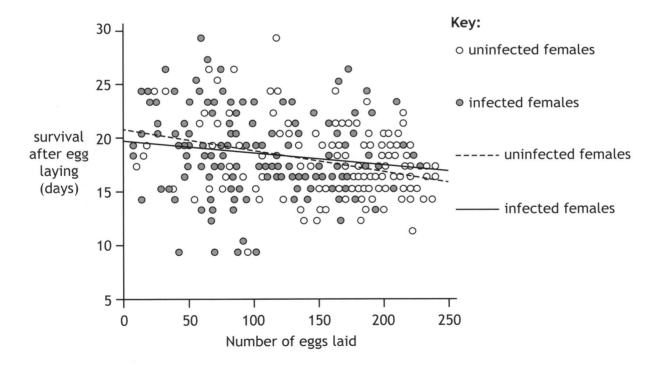

[BLANK PAGE]

DO NOT WRITE ON THIS PAGE

ADVANCED HIGHER

2017

18. Parthenogenesis is most likely to be common in environments with a

   A   warm climate and low parasite density

   B   warm climate and high parasite density

   C   cool climate and low parasite density

   D   cool climate and high parasite density.

19. Asexual reproduction is most likely to be a successful reproductive strategy in

   A   wide, stable niches

   B   narrow, stable niches

   C   wide, unstable niches

   D   narrow, unstable niches.

20. The black grouse male is larger and more brightly coloured than the female and competes with other males at leks.

   Which of the following pairs of features are characteristic of this species?

   A   Monogamy and sexual dimorphism

   B   Monogamy and reversed sexual dimorphism

   C   Polygamy and sexual dimorphism

   D   Polygamy and reversed sexual dimorphism

21. Which of the following conversions is catalysed by reverse transcriptase?

   A   RNA → DNA

   B   RNA → protein

   C   DNA → RNA

   D   DNA → protein

[Turn over

22. The figure represents the structure of a Zika virus.

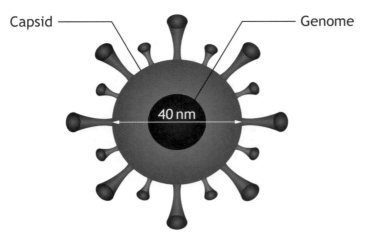

1,000,000 nm = 1 mm

Which row in the table describes the structure of a Zika virus?

	Capsid	Genome	Diameter (m)
A	Protein	Nucleic acid	40×10^{-6}
B	Protein	Nucleic acid	40×10^{-9}
C	Nucleic acid	Protein	40×10^{-6}
D	Nucleic acid	Protein	40×10^{-9}

23. Schistosomiasis in humans is caused by an

A   ectoparasitic arthropod

B   endoparasitic amoeba

C   endoparasitic nematode

D   endoparasitic platyhelminth.

24. Cholera is a disease which causes diarrhoea and is potentially fatal. It is transmitted through the consumption of food or water contaminated by the bacterium *Vibrio cholerae*. It often has a higher incidence in refugee camps than in the surrounding countryside.

Which of the following measures is **not** appropriate for reducing the incidence of cholera in refugee camps?

A   Improved vector control

B   Increased sanitation

C   Decreased population density

D   Reduced costs for cholera vaccines

25. The scatterplot shows the results obtained when life expectancy at birth was plotted against age at first reproduction for 24 species of mammals of different sizes.

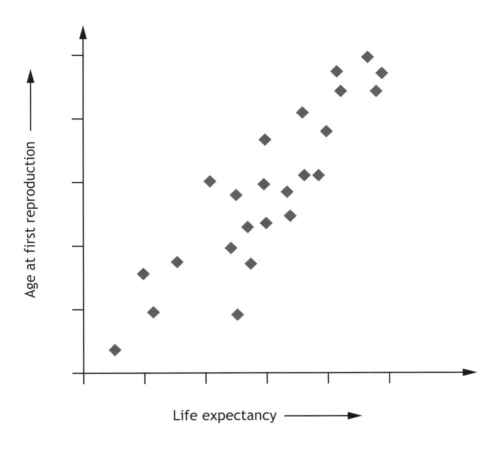

Which of the following conclusions can be drawn from the data?

A   An increase in life expectancy causes an increase in the age of first reproduction.

B   An increase in the age of first reproduction causes an increase in life expectancy.

C   Larger animals have longer life expectancy.

D   Life expectancy and age at first reproduction are correlated.

[END OF SECTION 1. NOW ATTEMPT THE QUESTIONS IN SECTION 2 OF YOUR QUESTION AND ANSWER BOOKLET.]

[BLANK PAGE]

DO NOT WRITE ON THIS PAGE

FOR OFFICIAL USE

National Qualifications 2017

Mark

X707/77/01

Biology
Section 1 — Answer Grid
and Section 2

TUESDAY, 23 MAY

9:00 AM — 11:30 AM

Fill in these boxes and read what is printed below.

Full name of centre

Town

Forename(s)

Surname

Number of seat

Date of birth

Day	Month	Year	Scottish candidate number

Total marks — 90

SECTION 1 — 25 marks

Attempt ALL questions.

Instructions for the completion of Section 1 are given on *Page two*.

SECTION 2 — 65 marks

Attempt ALL questions.

A Supplementary Sheet for Question 1 is enclosed inside the front cover of this question paper.

Write your answers clearly in the spaces provided in this booklet. Additional space for answers and rough work is provided at the end of this booklet. If you use this space you must clearly identify the question number you are attempting. Any rough work must be written in this booklet. You should score through your rough work when you have written your final copy.

Use **blue** or **black** ink.

Before leaving the examination room you must give this booklet to the Invigilator; if you do not, you may lose all the marks for this paper.

SECTION 1 — 25 marks

The questions for Section 1 are contained in the question paper X707/77/02.

Read these and record your answers on the answer grid on *Page three* opposite.

Use **blue** or **black** ink. Do NOT use gel pens or pencil.

1. The answer to each question is **either** A, B, C or D. Decide what your answer is, then fill in the appropriate bubble (see sample question below).

2. There is **only one correct** answer to each question.

3. Any rough working should be done on the additional space for answers and rough work at the end of this booklet.

Sample Question

The thigh bone is called the

     A   humerus

     B   femur

     C   tibia

     D   fibula.

The correct answer is **B** — femur. The answer **B** bubble has been clearly filled in (see below).

Changing an answer

If you decide to change your answer, cancel your first answer by putting a cross through it (see below) and fill in the answer you want. The answer below has been changed to **D**.

If you then decide to change back to an answer you have already scored out, put a tick (✓) to the **right** of the answer you want, as shown below:

                          or

SECTION 1 — Answer Grid

	A	B	C	D
1	○	○	○	○
2	○	○	○	○
3	○	○	○	○
4	○	○	○	○
5	○	○	○	○
6	○	○	○	○
7	○	○	○	○
8	○	○	○	○
9	○	○	○	○
10	○	○	○	○
11	○	○	○	○
12	○	○	○	○
13	○	○	○	○
14	○	○	○	○
15	○	○	○	○
16	○	○	○	○
17	○	○	○	○
18	○	○	○	○
19	○	○	○	○
20	○	○	○	○
21	○	○	○	○
22	○	○	○	○
23	○	○	○	○
24	○	○	○	○
25	○	○	○	○

[BLANK PAGE]

DO NOT WRITE ON THIS PAGE

[Turn over for next question

DO NOT WRITE ON THIS PAGE

MARKS | DO NOT WRITE IN THIS MARGIN

SECTION 2 — 65 marks

Attempt ALL questions

It should be noted that question 11 contains a choice

1. Read through the Supplementary Sheet for Question 1 before attempting this question.

   (a) **Refer to Figure 2 in the Supplementary Sheet for Question 1.**

   Describe the trend shown in Figure 2.   **1**

   _____

   _____

   _____

   (b) Describe the action of caspases in cell destruction.   **1**

   _____

   _____

   _____

   (c) **Refer to Figure 3 in the Supplementary Sheet for Question 1.**

   (i) Explain how the data supports the conclusion that the intrinsic pathway for apoptosis is triggered by the extract.   **2**

   _____

   _____

   _____

   _____

   (ii) Describe what the three negative values in Figure 3 indicate about the level of apoptosis in these treatments.   **1**

   _____

   _____

   _____

MARKS | DO NOT WRITE IN THIS MARGIN

1. **(continued)**

(d) **Refer to Figures 4A and 4B in the Supplementary Sheet for Question 1.**

(i) Calculate the percentage increase in the number of cells with 400 units of DNA in the cells treated with extract compared to the control cells.

Space for calculation

1

_____

(ii) It was concluded that the extract initiated cell cycle arrest at a checkpoint after DNA replication but prior to cell division in these cells.

Explain how the data in Figures 4A and 4B support this hypothesis. **2**

_____

_____

_____

_____

_____

[Turn over

2. The light sensitive layer at the back of the human eye is called the retina. It is able to detect light due to the presence of photoreceptor cells called cones and rods. There are three types of cone cells (blue, green and red) which are sensitive to different wavelengths of light as shown in Figure 1. Different wavelengths of light are perceived as different colours.

Figure 1

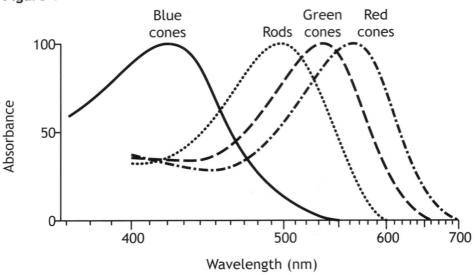

(a) (i) In cone cells, the light sensitive molecule retinal combines with a membrane protein to form photoreceptor proteins.

Name this membrane protein.   **1**

_____

(ii) One percent of human males do not have functional red cone cells, a colour vision deficiency called *protanopia*.

Affected individuals would perceive a red object reflecting light of a wavelength of 670 nm as black.

Use Figure 1 to explain this observation.   **1**

_____

_____

_____

MARKS | DO NOT WRITE IN THIS MARGIN

2. **(continued)**

(b) Rod cells are more sensitive than cone cells at low light intensities.

State how this sensitivity is achieved.   1

_____

_____

(c) Most birds have four types of cone cells.

Name the additional wavelength range to which these organisms are sensitive.   1

_____

[Turn over

3. Cortisol is a hydrophobic signalling molecule, produced by the human adrenal gland, that affects a number of different tissues in response to stress. It has a role in increasing blood sugar levels, in suppressing the immune system, and in promoting the metabolism of fats, proteins, and carbohydrates.

   (a) (i) Cortisol is a steroid hormone.

   Describe the mechanism by which this type of signalling molecule causes an effect within the target cell.

   2

   _____

   _____

   _____

   _____

   _____

   (ii) Suggest a way in which cortisol might have different effects in different tissues.

   1

   _____

   _____

   _____

MARKS | DO NOT WRITE IN THIS MARGIN

3.   (continued)

(b) Addison's disease is a disorder in which the adrenal glands do not produce sufficient cortisol. One test for this disease is to give the patient an injection of a hormone called ACTH, which stimulates the adrenal gland to release cortisol. In a healthy person, cortisol levels should rise by at least 70 µg per litre after 30 minutes **and** 110 µg per litre after 60 minutes.

The graph shows the results of this test on three patients who were investigated for Addison's disease.

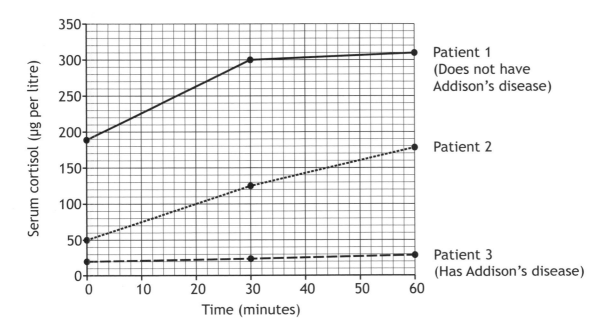

State the diagnosis that would be appropriate for Patient 2, using data to justify your answer.   1

_____

_____

_____

[Turn over

MARKS | DO NOT WRITE IN THIS MARGIN

4. The diagram shows how two types of enzyme can be involved in controlling the activity of a protein in response to the presence of a signalling molecule within the cell (intracellular signal molecule). Intracellular signalling molecules are often produced as a result of extracellular signals received by cell-surface receptors.

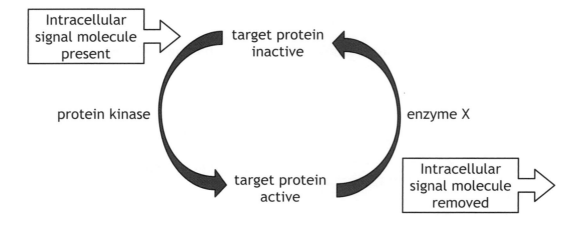

(a) (i) Explain how the action of protein kinase can switch a target protein from inactive to active.   **1**

_____

_____

_____

(ii) Name the type of enzyme represented by enzyme X.   **1**

_____

(iii) Explain the importance of the system being able to return the target protein to its inactive state.   **1**

_____

_____

MARKS | DO NOT WRITE IN THIS MARGIN

4.   (continued)

(b)   Protein kinase A (PKA) is an enzyme that is involved in this type of signalling. To test the hypothesis that PKA is found in a variety of cell types, cell extracts were prepared from different cell types and the proteins in the extracts separated by electrophoresis in a gel. The proteins were blotted onto a solid support and an antibody recognising PKA (anti-PKA antibody) was used to detect the presence of PKA.

(i)   Describe how protein electrophoresis is used to separate proteins.   1

_____

_____

_____

(ii)   Explain how the anti-PKA antibody would be used to detect the presence of PKA.   2

_____

_____

_____

_____

[Turn over

MARKS | DO NOT WRITE IN THIS MARGIN

5. The water vole (*Arvicola amphibius*) was common in Scotland but has declined markedly in recent years due to habitat loss and predation by American mink (*Neovison vison*).

A survey was carried out to estimate the population of water voles on a Scottish river system by counting the number of latrines (droppings sites) on a river bank at the water's edge. Water vole latrines are created as part of a territorial behaviour where a water vole will revisit the same site over and over again to deposit its droppings.

Water vole

American mink

(a) Suggest one reason why counting latrines is an appropriate indirect sampling technique for water voles.   1

_____

_____

(b) The survey team worked on a total of 518 km, using survey sites of 500 m at 5 km intervals along the river system. The number of latrines per kilometre of waterways was counted.

Name the type of sampling used.   1

_____

MARKS | DO NOT WRITE IN THIS MARGIN

5. (continued)

(c) All surveys were conducted in June, July and August of the same year. There was heavy rainfall for three days in August. Any survey site too deep to walk into was omitted. The remains of one water vole that had been preyed upon were discovered at one survey site. Of the 92 sites sampled, only one site showed any latrines.

Identify one aspect of the experimental design that shows:

(i) High reliability;

1

_____

_____

(ii) Low reliability.

1

_____

_____

(d) It was concluded that the water vole population on this river had become extremely low due to predation by American mink.

Give two reasons why this may **not** be a valid conclusion.

2

1 _____

_____

2 _____

_____

[Turn over

6. The mechanism of sex determination is not the same for all species.

(a) In most mammals the sex of the organism is determined by its genotype.

Describe how genetic control determines the phenotype of maleness in **mammals.**

1

(b) In some reptile species the sex of offspring is environmentally rather than genetically controlled.

Describe how an environmental factor can influence the sex ratio of offspring in such species.

1

(c) Diabetes insipidus is a condition characterised by the production of an excessive volume of dilute urine. An hereditary form of the disease in humans is the result of an X-linked mutation in the gene coding for the receptor for the hormone ADH. The mutated allele (X^a) is recessive to the normal allele (X^A).

(i) Explain why males are more likely to be affected by diabetes insipidus than females.

1

(ii) Explain why carrier females are usually not affected by diabetes insipidus even though they carry a mutated copy of the gene.

2

MARKS | DO NOT WRITE IN THIS MARGIN

6. **(c)** **(continued)**

(iii) A man who is not affected by diabetes insipidus has a partner who is a carrier.

State the proportion of their sons that would be predicted to have the condition.   **1**

Space for working

_____ %

[Turn over

7. Students observed a group of California sea lions (*Zalophus californianus*) that were situated on a rocky outcrop off the coast of California. During each observation period, ten sea lions were observed for six minutes each. The sea lions were watched from a distance using binoculars. The checklist was used as a reference when recording the behaviours observed.

California sea lion

Behaviour	Description of behaviour
grooming	Licking, smoothing self with tongue, scratching
observing	Sitting up on flippers looking around
resting	Lying down with some head raising, barking or yawning
movement, aggressive	Barking, aggressive charging or chasing
movement, non-aggressive	Moving for better position on rock
other	Behaviours not specified above

(a) State the term used for a behavioural checklist of this kind.   1

_____

(b) As they observed the sea lions the students noted the time at which each new behaviour started.

Describe how the data could be used to construct a time budget.   1

_____

_____

MARKS | DO NOT WRITE IN THIS MARGIN

7. **(continued)**

(c) One student noted, "Sometimes the sea lions tried to annoy each other."

Explain why anthropomorphic statements such as this should be avoided in behavioural studies.

1

_____

_____

_____

(d) Observing the sea lions from a distance made distinguishing some details of behaviour difficult.

Suggest an improvement to the method, other than direct observation, that would reduce this source of error.

1

_____

_____

[Turn over

MARKS | DO NOT WRITE IN THIS MARGIN

8. "So sex exists to keep parasites at bay." (Lane, 2009)

With reference to the Red Queen hypothesis, discuss the importance of sexual reproduction in defence against parasites.

5

_____

_____

_____

_____

_____

_____

_____

_____

_____

_____

[Turn over for next question

DO NOT WRITE ON THIS PAGE

MARKS | DO NOT WRITE IN THIS MARGIN

9. *Acraea encedon* is a butterfly found in tropical Africa.

Females of this species can be one of two types: either producing broods that are entirely female or producing broods that have males and females in an approximate 1:1 sex ratio. One hypothesis proposed to explain the all-female broods was that bacteria inherited from the mother kill male embryos only.

(a) Explain how antibiotics that kill bacteria could be used in a controlled trial to test this hypothesis.   **2**

_____

_____

_____

_____

(b) Research has shown that the rapid evolution of male-killing bacteria from non-male-killing strains has been enabled by horizontal gene transfer.

Explain what is meant by "horizontal gene transfer".   **1**

_____

_____

MARKS | DO NOT WRITE IN THIS MARGIN

9.   (continued)

(c)   Some populations of the butterfly are extremely female-biased with over 90% being infected with this bacterium. These females form lekking swarms at landmarks. This has been described as *sex-role-reversal*. Butterfly populations that are not female-biased do not have lekking swarms.

Suggest the purpose of the lekking swarms and explain why they are only found in female-biased populations of the butterfly.   2

_____

_____

_____

_____

(d)   Other sex-role-reversed mating systems are usually associated with males investing more than females in offspring, but this is not the case with *A. encedon*.

Suggest **one** way in which males might demonstrate greater reproductive investment than females in a sex-role-reversed mating system.   1

_____

_____

[Turn over

MARKS | DO NOT WRITE IN THIS MARGIN

10. The graph shows the number of measles notifications (reported cases) since 1950 and vaccination rates since 1970.

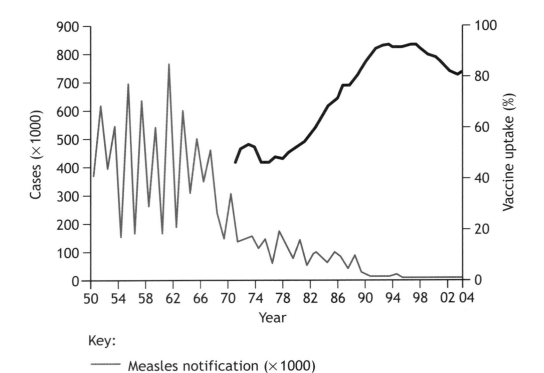

Key:

——— Measles notification (×1000)

——— Vaccine uptake (%)

(a) State the term used to describe the study of data concerned with the outbreak and spread of infectious disease.

1

_____

(b) Describe the pattern of measles notifications prior to the introduction of vaccination.

1

_____

_____

(c) Describe the correlation suggested by the graph.

1

_____

_____

MARKS | DO NOT WRITE IN THIS MARGIN

10. (continued)

(d) The MMR vaccine was introduced in 1988 to combat the infectious viral diseases of measles, mumps and rubella. In 1998, a report, published in a peer reviewed medical journal, claimed to establish a link between the MMR vaccine and the disorder known as autism.

(i) Explain what is meant by the term "peer reviewed". **1**

(ii) Although criticised heavily and eventually discredited, this research led to a considerable reduction in the number of children being vaccinated. In some areas, such as Swansea in South Wales, vaccination rates fell as low as 67·5%. Over the same period, a huge increase in the number of measles notifications occurred in that area.

Account for the spread of measles in the Swansea epidemic. **1**

(iii) Explain how the events in Swansea confirm that the graph not only shows correlation but also shows causation. **1**

(e) The World Health Organisation (WHO) recommends 95% of children should be immunised (vaccinated) against measles in order to protect all.

State the term used to describe this WHO threshold. **1**

[Turn over for next question

MARKS | DO NOT WRITE IN THIS MARGIN

11. Answer **either A or B** in the space below and on *Page twenty-seven*.

A   Discuss the role of amino acid R-groups in:

(i)   the determination of tertiary structure of proteins;   **3**

(ii) influencing the location of proteins within cells.   **6**

OR

B   Discuss cell membranes under the following headings:

(i)   the phospholipid bilayer as a selective barrier;   **2**

(ii) types of transport proteins and their functions.   **7**

MARKS | DO NOT WRITE IN THIS MARGIN

SPACE FOR ANSWER FOR QUESTION 11

[END OF QUESTION PAPER]

MARKS DO NOT WRITE IN THIS MARGIN

ADDITIONAL SPACE FOR ANSWERS AND ROUGH WORK

MARKS | DO NOT WRITE IN THIS MARGIN

ADDITIONAL SPACE FOR ANSWERS AND ROUGH WORK

Page twenty-nine

[BLANK PAGE]

DO NOT WRITE ON THIS PAGE

AH

National
Qualifications
2017

X707/77/11

**Biology
Supplementary Sheet**

TUESDAY, 23 MAY
9:00 AM – 11:30 AM

Supplementary Sheet for Question 1

1. There are two main pathways of programmed cell death (apoptosis): *intrinsic* (from within the cell) and *extrinsic* (from outside the cell).

Figure 1 summarises some of the main features of the two pathways.

Figure 1

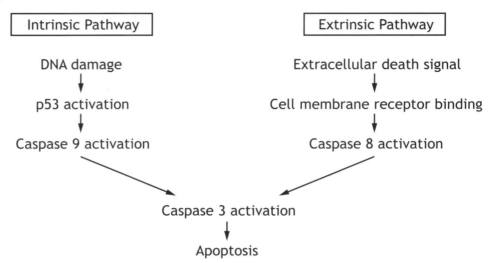

Apoptosis is deregulated in many tumours, resulting in uncontrolled cell division despite the presence of significant DNA damage. One strategy for the discovery of new anti-cancer drugs has been to examine traditional medicinal herbs.

A study was carried out to investigate the effect of an extract of the wild ginger plant, *Asiasari radix*, on the initiation of apoptosis in colon cancer cells.

Colon cancer cells were treated with this extract and then assessed for the presence of apoptotic cells. The percentage increase in cells undergoing apoptosis was calculated by comparing the level of apoptosis in treated cells with that in untreated controls as shown in Figure 2.

Figure 2

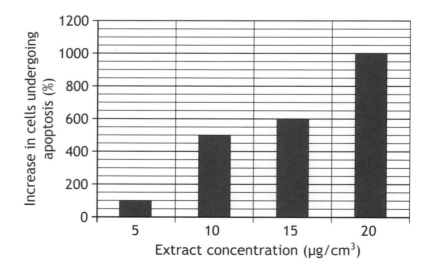

1. **(continued)**

To investigate the involvement of caspases in this process of apoptosis, the experiment was repeated using a single dose of extract ($10\,\mu g/cm^3$) but with the addition of a variety of caspase inhibitors (drugs known to prevent the activation of one or more caspases). Inhibitors used included an inhibitor known to prevent activation of all caspases (all ci) and individual inhibitors of caspase 3 (ci 3), caspase 8 (ci 8) and caspase 9 (ci 9). Percentage changes in the number of cells undergoing apoptosis compared to untreated cancer cells are shown in Figure 3.

Figure 3

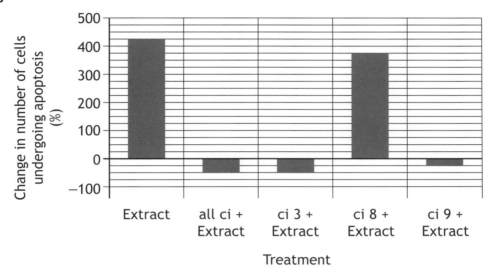

The distribution of the cancer cells across the different phases of the cell cycle was then investigated by measuring the DNA content of the cells. Cultures of cells were treated with $10\,\mu g/cm^3$ extract or left untreated for 24 hours as a control and then the DNA content of 10,000 cells was analysed for each cell culture. Results for treated cells are shown in Figure 4A and for control cells in Figure 4B. DNA content is displayed with arbitrary units where 200 units represents the DNA content of a non-dividing diploid cell.

Figure 4A

Figure 4B

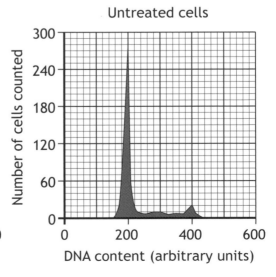

[BLANK PAGE]

DO NOT WRITE ON THIS PAGE

ADVANCED HIGHER

Answers

ADVANCED HIGHER BIOLOGY
2015 SPECIMEN QUESTION PAPER

Section 1

Question	Response	Mark
1.	A	1
2.	C	1
3.	B	1
4.	A	1
5.	D	1
6.	B	1
7.	C	1
8.	A	1
9.	C	1
10.	A	1
11.	C	1
12.	D	1
13.	C	1
14.	D	1
15.	A	1
16.	B	1
17.	C	1
18.	C	1
19.	B	1
20.	D	1
21.	D	1
22.	B	1
23.	A	1
24.	D	1
25.	C	1

Section 2

Question			Expected response	Max mark	Additional guidance
1.	(a)		Proteome	1	
	(b)		• Drosha not working • miRNA/precursor not processed/cut • No (micro)RNA strand for RISC OR RISC can't bind (m)RNA • (RNA) interference reduced/translation is left on	2	Any two
	(c)	(i)	Cell growth/cell increases in mass	1	
		(ii)	62·5	1	
		(iii)	More KO cells in G1 and fewer in S (and G2 + M) (1) Differences are significant (only) in G1 and S/error bars don't overlap in G1 and S (1) OR If comparing only G1 bars or only S bars, then must point out significant difference (1)	2	Comparison can be made via data but data must be correct

	(d)	(i)	(After induction of differentiation)
			• in KO cells it is (generally) lower than normal cells
			• it increases in normal cells (over time)
			• in KO cells + one from below
			  — no trend
			  — decreases from day 8
			  — increases (to day 8) then decreases
			(It = expression = level of marker)
				1	Any one

		(ii)	• In normal cells, as differentiation increases self-renewal decreases **OR** converse (must link the two graphs/processes) • In KO/abnormal cells, **both** processes decrease after day 8 • in KO/abnormal cells, **both** processes increase to day 8 • in KO/abnormal cells, self-renewal remains higher and differentiation remains lower **than normal**	2	Any two
2.	(a)		• GABA is a ligand/substance that can bind to protein • The channel is a protein that opens in response to GABA/ligand binding • Chloride passes through the protein when GABA is bound	2	Any two
	(b)		Transduction	1	
	(c)	(i)	Chloride movement is (generally) greater at any GABA conc. if drug present	1	
		(ii)	Changes the conformation of the GABA site	1	
		(iii)	(Make the cell more negative inside so) increase the membrane potential	1	

Question			Expected response	Max mark	Additional guidance
3.	(a)		Concentration of ATP solution	1	
	(b)	(i)	Freshness of meat/whether meat has been frozen/ temperature of storage/incubation time/time before measurement/thickness of strip	1	Any one
		(ii)	• Storage of meat may cause damage to muscle proteins so muscle contraction would be less with less fresh meat • Freezing meat may damage muscle fibres so less contraction would be measured • Freezing meat may preserve muscle proteins so more contraction would be measured • As storage temperature increases protein damage may increase so less muscle contraction would be measured • Increasing incubation time/time before measurement will give more time for ATP to diffuse so more muscle contraction would be measured • ATP will diffuse more slowly through thicker strips which could mean the solution does not reach all the fibres so less contraction will be measured	1	Any one Explanation of effect must match with chosen confounding variable
	(c)		Not reliable (1) No independent replication/whole experiment was only carried out once OR Only one measurement for each chop at each concentration of ATP (1)	2	
	(d)		Negative control	1	
	(e)		May have prevented a representative sample being selected	1	
4.	(a)		The training will have no effect on GLUT 4 content of muscle	1	
	(b)		ND UT is baseline GLUT 4 **and** training does not produce significant increase (1) D UT is (significantly) lower GLUT 4 than baseline and exercise generates significant increase (1)	2	
	(c)		Type 1 diabetes is failure to produce insulin whereas type 2 diabetes is loss of insulin receptor function/ failure to respond to insulin	1	
5.	(a)		Hydrophobic	1	
	(b)		Thyroxine receptor protein is blocking transcription/ thyroxine binding removes repression of genes (1) More NaKATPase in membrane so more energy expenditure/higher metabolic rate (1)	2	
	(c)	(i)	People need to be treated for several weeks before metabolic rate reaches normal	1	
		(ii)	Starting metabolic rate is different for each individual	1	

Question			Expected response	Max mark	Additional guidance
6.	(a)		Retinal	1	
	(b)		• Excited rhodopsin activates G protein which in turn activates many enzyme molecules • Enzyme molecules cause closure of ion channels/catalyse the removal of molecules that keep channels open • Inward leakage of positive ions/Na$^+$ and Ca$^+$ is halted so membrane potential increases • Hyperpolarisation/increasing charge stimulates nerve impulse	2	Any two
	(c)		Wide range of wavelengths absorbed/high degree of amplification from single photon	1	
7.	(a)		Men have one allele of the haemophilia gene whereas women have two alleles (of the haemophilia gene) (1) Recessive allele causing haemophilia not masked in men (1)	2	
	(b)		Daughter 100% (1) Son 50% (1)	2	
	(c)	(i)	Prevents a double dose of gene products (coded by the X chromosome) that might disrupt cellular function	1	
		(ii)	Inactivation of X chromosomes is random so this patient must have (by chance) more cells that have inactivated the unaffected allele/fewer cells that inactivated the affected allele	1	
8.			• homologous chromosomes pair (during meiosis I) • breakage and re-joining of DNA strands • at chiasmata • shuffles sections of DNA between homologous chromosomes • allows the recombination of alleles • (as) linked genes are separated	4	Any four
9.	(a)	(i)	Does not itself actively transmit parasite to another species	1	
		(ii)	Waterborne dispersal stage	1	
	(b)		• Mimic host antigens to evade detection • Modify host immune response to reduce chances of destruction • Antigenic variation allows rapid evolution to overcome host immune cell clonal selection	1	Any one
	(c)		Co-evolution of related species that interact frequently/closely (1) Change in traits of one species acts as a selection pressure on the other species (1)	2	

Question			Expected response	Max mark	Additional guidance
10.	(a)		300%	1	
	(b)	(i)	Reduction in abundance of named species due to increase in seal population/physical damage/trampling (1) Increase in abundance of *Prasiola crispa* due to reduced competition for space/greater tolerance of trampling (1)	2	
		(ii)	Loss of plants gives areas of bare rock OR Not all plant species counted	1	
	(c)	(i)	Carried out in a way that minimises impact on environment OR Consideration of rare/vulnerable species	1	
		(ii)	Population being sampled is split into sub-populations	1	
11.	A		1. Immune surveillance by white blood cells 2. T lymphocytes recognise antigens from pathogen 3. Antigens (from pathogen) displayed on the surface of infected cells 4. T lymphocytes destroy infected cells 5. T lymphocytes induce apoptosis 6. Phagocytes present antigens to lymphocytes 7. B lymphocytes produce specific antibodies 8. T lymphocytes/B lymphocytes amplified by clonal selection 9. A different lymphocyte is produced/selected for each antigen 10. Long-term survival of some members of T lymphocyte/B lymphocyte clones 11. Surviving lymphocytes act as immunological memory cells	8	Any eight
	B		1. Female choice assesses male fitness 2. Females assess honest signals (to assess fitness) 3. Fitness explained in terms of advantageous genes/low parasite burdens 4. Display behaviour of lekking species 5. Successful strategies of dominant and satellite males (in lekking species) 6. Example of lekking behaviour described 7. Male—male rivalry: large size/weaponry 8. Increases access to females through conflict 9. Behaviour of sneaker males 10. Importance of sign stimuli and fixed action pattern in birds/fish 11. Example of sign stimuli and fixed action pattern described	8	Any eight

ADVANCED HIGHER BIOLOGY 2016

Section 1

Question	Answer	Max mark
1.	D	1
2.	A	1
3.	A	1
4.	B	1
5.	C	1
6.	B	1
7.	B	1
8.	C	1
9.	C	1
10.	D	1
11.	B	1
12.	A	1
13.	B	1
14.	A	1
15.	B	1
16.	D	1
17.	D	1
18.	D	1
19.	C	1
20.	B	1
21.	A	1
22.	C	1
23.	C	1
24.	D	1
25.	C	1

Section 2

Question			Expected answer(s)	Max mark	Additional guidance
1.	(a)	(i)	Statement relating to quartiles e.g. 25% lay more than/UQ is 200 eggs e.g. 50% lay more than 170 eggs **OR** Median value is 170 eggs (laid) e.g. 75% lay more than/LQ is 125 eggs e.g. 50% lay between 125 and 200 OR Equivalents 'in opposite direction' OR Range of eggs (laid) is between 20 and 240/range of eggs (laid) is 220 OR Minimum and maximum values are 20 and 240 eggs (laid) OR No. of eggs (laid) is very variable **(Any two)**	2	• If no reference to 'eggs' deduct one mark only **Not:** • average = median • 'average median'
		(ii)	Mean number of eggs laid/it is higher (than the median) OR Mean is greater than 90	1	
		(iii)	(Infection) reduces (fecundity)	1	Fecundity = no. of eggs laid
	(b)	(i)	Error bars do not overlap	1	
		(ii)	Increases (chance of)/more time for transmission (of parasite) OR More time for (parasite) reproduction	1	Transmission = spread/passed on to host **Not:** • allows transmission • reference to humans **Ignore:** • reference to intermediate/definitive host

Question			Expected answer(s)	Max mark	Additional guidance
	(c)	(i)	Negative correlation between survival and the number of eggs laid OR Mosquitoes that lay smaller numbers of eggs live longer **(1)** Relationship is more negatively correlated in uninfected mosquitoes OR As fecundity increases the decrease in longevity is greater in uninfected mosquitoes **(1)**	2	Accept converse. Accept converse. Accept converse.
		(ii)	not reliable because many points lie far from the line OR reliable because a large sample was used	1	
2.	(a)		(Serum) provides <u>growth factor(s)</u>	1	**Negates:** • nutrients
	(b)	(i)	110,000	1	
		(ii)	Dead cells are not distinguished from live cells (unless stained) OR Small cells difficult to locate OR Numbers obtained are only an estimate OR Time-consuming OR Clumping of cells **(Any one)**	1	
	(c)		(Thin sections of) tissue OR Whole/unicellular organism OR Parts of organism **(Any one)**	1	**Not:** • named example of organism • named examples of parts of organisms
	(d)		**Replacement** (with another biological system, eg cell culture) OR **Reduction** (in no. used) OR **Refinement** (re techniques) **(Any one)**	1	Any description/ example should relate to one of the concepts.

Question			Expected answer(s)	Max mark	Additional guidance
3.	(a)		Level/quantity of interferon (beta-1b)	1	interferon beta-1b = drug
	(b)		Allows (overall) effect of drug on (whole) organism/ body to be observed OR Allows (possible) side effects to be seen OR Shows effects on non-target cells OR Nerve cells difficult to grow *in vitro* **(Any one)**	1	**Not:** • Reference to ecological validity
	(c)		Provides results in the absence of the drug OR Gives baseline against which effect of drug can be measured/compared OR Allows comparison between drug and absence of drug OR Shows drug was responsible for effect OR Allows measurement of psychological effect (of treatment) **(Any one)**	1	**Not:** • Presence of drug = treatment
	(d)		Patients may not (remember to) take drug OR Patients may not inject/administer drug correctly/ effeactively OR May be different numbers in the three groups OR Some patients pulled out (before completing trial) OR Not all patients were (MRI) scanned/no scan data for 0·05 mg OR Patient self-assessment (is subjective/may be recorded incorrectly) OR Small sample size **(Any one)**	1	

Question			Expected answer(s)	Max mark	Additional guidance
	(e)		Informed consent OR Permission from patient to use results/data OR Right to withdraw OR Confidentiality OR Justification of research OR (Consider possible) risk/harm/side effects to patient (Any one)	1	
	(f)		Drug prevents/reduces **worsening** of MS/symptoms OR Higher levels of drug more effective OR Drug reduces **new** nerve damage (Any two)	2	Interferon beta-1b = drug **Not only** reference to single data point for conclusions based on Table 1. **FOR Table 2:** **Accept** reference to single data point but **NOT** dose related trend.
4.	(a)		Hydrophobic/Non-polar	1	
	(b)		Alpha-helix Turn	1	
	(c)		Binding (to one subunit of one oxygen) makes the binding of other oxygen more likely	1	Correct reference to affinity change for binding/release of oxygen. **Not:** • binding to other Hbs
	(d)		At low pressures (below 15–20) there is no difference OR Comparison of (maximum) O_2 saturation at 90/100 pressure units (95 vs 50%)　(1) At high pressures (15–20 upwards) increase for normal is greater than for sickle cell　(1)	2	

Question			Expected answer(s)	Max mark	Additional guidance
	(e)		Valine has no charge (on R group) so (haemoglobin) molecules don't repel (one another) OR Hydrophobic interactions occur between (R groups of) valines (causing clumping) OR Glutamic acid has a charge (on R group) so (haemoglobin) molecules repel **(Any one)**	1	Interaction between non polar R groups of valines is equivalent to hydrophobic interactions between valines.
5.			1. Cell division requires remodelling of cytoskeleton 2. Spindle fibres made of microtubules 3. Composed of tubulin 4. (Composed of) hollow/ straight rods/cylinders/tubes **Maximum 2 marks from 1 to 4** 5. Attach to chromosomes/chromatids/centromeres/ kinetochores 6. Radiate from centrosome/microtubule organising centre/MTOC 7. Spindle fibres contract/shorten 8. Separate chromatids/(homologous) chromosomes **Maximum 2 marks from 5 to 8**	4	**Pt 6** Radiate = extend = grow = originate = made **Allow** Radiate from centriole but **NOT** Grow from/made by centriole.
6.	(a)		Maintaining osmotic balance OR Generation of ion (concentration) gradient AND one from: • For glucose symport (in small intestine) • In kidney tubules • For maintenance of resting potential (in cells/ neurons)	1	**Not:** • Maintain osmotic gradient
	(b)		Phosphorylation/conformational change (of pump) **(1)** **Lowers** affinity (for Na^+ ions) **(1)**	2	Conformational change must relate to ATP binding/ phosphorylation.
	(c)		Prevents binding of K^+ ions **(1)** Preventing de-phosphorylation OR Prevents (reversal of) conformational change OR Affinity for Na^+ ions (remains) low **(1)**	2	

Question			Expected answer(s)	Max mark	Additional guidance
7.	(a)	(i)	Aquaporin-(2)/AQP(2)	1	
		(ii)	Signal transduction	1	
	(b)	(i)	Urine output >3·5 litres (per day) on days without treatment/on day 1/2/5/6 OR Correct calculation of urine output per kg body mass on day 1/2/5/6 AND Stating value >0·05 litres/kg/day	1	Units required. e.g. from: day 1: 10·5/70 = ~0·15 day 2: 10/70 = 0·14 day 5: 8/70 = ~0·11 day 6: 9/70 = ~0·13
		(ii)	Urine production was <3·5 litres/<0·05 litres per kg on day 3/4 OR Urine production was <3·5 litres per day/<0·05 litres per kg per day during treatment OR Correct calculation showing urine output reduced to < critical level on day 3/4 **(Any one)**	1	'on day 3/4' **equivalent to** 'during treatment'
		(iii)	Failure to produce/lack of ADH	1	
8.	(a)		Gamete mother cell	1	
	(b)	(i)	Crossing over (at chiasmata) OR Breakage and rejoining of DNA/chromatids (at chiasmata) **(1)** (Leads to) exchange of DNA/alleles between (homologous) chromosomes OR New combinations of/recombination of alleles (of linked genes) **(1)**	2	
		(ii)	Independent assortment	1	
9.	(a)		(Much) greater proportion (of Mrcaru lizard's diet) is plant matter	1	
	(b)	(i)	(Mrcaru) lizards have micro-organisms to break down plant matter/greater bite force **(1)** These individuals AND are (better) **adapted** to new environment/eating plant matter/digesting plant matter OR have selective advantage/increased fitness **(1)**	2	suited ≠ adapted Accept description of *selective advantage*.

Question			Expected answer(s)	Max mark	Additional guidance
		(ii)	Short(er) generation time OR Warm(er) environment/climate/high(er) temperature OR High(er) selection pressure OR High(er) mutation rate OR Sexual reproduction/horizontal gene transfer **(Any one)**	1	
	(c)		Same mean as population as a whole OR Same degree of variation about/deviation from mean as the population (as a whole) **(Any one)**	1	
10.	(a)		Sexual dimorphism	1	
	(b)	(i)	Males gather/compete in (communal) area/lek (to display) AND Females assess/choose male OR To allow female choice	1	
		(ii)	(Display) increases **male's** chance of mating/passing on genes/reproducing OR (Display) increases **male's** breeding success	1	
		(iii)	(Surviving) offspring have increased fitness/more favourable characteristics OR High/greater number of surviving offspring	1	Characteristics = traits = genes = alleles
	(c)	(i)	(Sound) allows communication over (long) distance OR (Sound) overcomes difficulty of limited visibility OR (Sound) allows communication in spite of forest/trees limiting visual signals OR Allows female to locate male(s)/lek **(Any one)**	1	
		(ii)	(Dishonest as fake hoots) not indicating male mating success/fitness OR (Dishonest as fake hoots emitted when) females not present/no mating occurring	1	

Question			Expected answer(s)	Max mark	Additional guidance
11.	A	(i)	Costs/benefits of sexual reproduction: 1. Males/50% are unable to produce offspring OR Only females/50% able to produce offspring Only half of (each parent's) genome passed on (to offspring) 2. Disrupts successful (parental) genomes OR (Combinations of) beneficial alleles/traits lost 3. Increases (genetic) variation 4. (Variation) allows evolution/adaptation (in response to changing environment) 5. (Variation allows organism) to keep running in the Red Queen arms race (e.g. between parasite and host) **Maximum 4 marks from 1 to 6**	9	Produce offspring = reproduce Genome = genes = alleles = DNA = genetic information **Pt 2—NOT:** • traits
		(ii)	Asexual reproduction as a successful reproductive strategy: a. Successful genome passed on b. In narrow stable niches c. When recolonizing disturbed habitats d. Vegetative cloning in plants OR description of suitable example e. Parthenogenesis (in animals) OR description of example f. (Parthenogenesis) where parasite burden is low/climate is cool/parasite diversity is low g. (In organisms using asexual reproduction) horizontal gene transfer allows exchange of genetic material/increased variation h. Example of horizontal gene transfer **Maximum 5 marks from points a to h**		
	B	(i)	Difficulties involved in treatment and control: 1. Endoparasite defined as living within host 2. Rapid antigen change/high antigenic variation 3. Vaccines difficult to design/ produce 4. (Some) parasites difficult to culture (in vitro/laboratory) 5. Similarity between host and parasite **metabolism** 6. Difficult to find drugs only toxic to parasite 7. Difficulty associated with vector control OR Indirect transmission 8. Transmission rate high in tropical climate/overcrowded situations 9. Overcrowding (can occur) in refugee camps/rapidly growing cities (in LEDCs) 10. Difficult/expensive to improve sanitation **Maximum 7 marks from 1 to 10**	9	**Pt 8.** **Accept:** • Spread more rapidly • Overcrowding = high population density
		(ii)	Benefits of improved parasite control to human populations: a. Reduction in child mortality b. Improvements in child development/intelligence c. Body uses more resources for growth/development **Maximum 2 marks from a to c**		

ADVANCED HIGHER BIOLOGY 2017

Section 1

Question	Answer	Max mark
1.	B	1
2.	C	1
3.	C	1
4.	D	1
5.	A	1
6.	C	1
7.	B	1
8.	D	1
9.	A	1
10.	A	1
11.	D	1
12.	B	1
13.	A	1
14.	C	1
15.	C	1
16.	B	1
17.	B	1
18.	C	1
19.	B	1
20.	C	1
21.	A	1
22.	B	1
23.	D	1
24.	A	1
25.	D	1

Section 2

Question			Expected answer(s)	Max mark	Additional guidance
1.	(a)		As extract concentration increases, the (percentage) increase in cells undergoing apoptosis increases	1	Ignore data
	(b)		Digest/break down proteins. **OR** Are proteases/proteinases. **OR** Caspases activate other caspases/ DNAases/aspase cascade.	1	
	(c)	(i)	ci8 (+ extract) gives similar levels of apoptosis to extract alone **OR** ci8 (+ extract) has little/no effect on apoptosis (1) ci9 (+ extract) results in decrease in apoptosis (1)	2	Correct use of numbers acceptable e.g. ci 9 + extract results in 25% decrease
		(ii)	(Level undergoing apoptosis) is lower than in the untreated cells/control	1	
	(d)	(i)	350 (%)	1	
		(ii)	Cells with 400 units of DNA have replicated (but not divided). **OR** In 4A/treated cells 400 peak is higher than 200. **AND** Shows cells have replicated/not divided/arrested at G2. **OR** In 4B/untreated cells 200 peak is higher than 400. **AND** Shows cells have divided. (1) Peak/number of cells with DNA content of 400 units is greater in 4A/treated cells than in 4B/ untreated cells. (1)	2	
2.	(a)	(i)	Opsin/photopsin (I, II or III)	1	
		(ii)	670 nm/it would be beyond the range of detection of all photoreceptors/green (and blue) cones (and rods).	1	**Accept:** • **Only** red cones detect light at this wavelength/ 670nm so no light detected. • Detected = absorbed perceived. **Not:** No light absorbed = v low absorption

Question			Expected answer(s)	Max mark	Additional guidance
	(b)		High (degree of) amplification.	1	**Accept:** Description of amplification pathway, e.g. (one photon stimulates/activates) hundreds/many G proteins which stimulate many enzymes
	(c)		UV/ultraviolet.	1	**Not:** numbers
3.	(a)	(i)	Cortisol/it diffuses through cell membrane. (1) Binds to receptor which switches transcription on/off. **OR** Binds to a transcription factor. (1)	2	**Accept:** Passes through = crosses = diffusion Alters gene expression = switches transcription on/off
		(ii)	(Different tissues will have) different responses **to receptor binding.** **OR** (Different tissues will have) different signal transduction pathways. **OR** Different genes switched off/on (in different tissues). **OR** There may be different cortisol receptors.	1	
	(b)		Does not have Addison's; Patient 2 cortisol increases by 75 µg per litre at 30 min and increases by 125 µg per litre at 60 min.	1	**Accept:** • Patient 2 increases by 75 µg per litre at 30 mins and a further 50 µg per litre at 60 mins. W.r.t between 30 and 60 mins • range of 125-130 range of 50-55. **Need:** Correct units (µg per litre) at least once.
4.	(a)	(i)	Kinase adds a phosphate to/phosphorylates (target protein; protein changes conformation).	1	
		(ii)	(Protein) phosphatase.	1	
		(iii)	So that sensitivity to the signal is restored. **OR** So that the (target) protein can respond again.	1	

Question			Expected answer(s)	Max mark	Additional guidance
	(b)	(i)	Charge/current (flowing through buffer) separates proteins (in gel) on the basis of size/mass/shape/charge.	1	
		(ii)	Antibody labelled (fluorescence/enzyme). (1) Fluorescence/colour/label detected if antibody has bound to PKA (showing its presence). (1)	2	**Accept:** Colour change = colour detected.
5.	(a)		Species may be elusive. **OR** Disturbance/harm/impact is minimised.	1	
	(b)		Systematic (sampling).	1	
	(c)	(i)	Long length of river sampled. **OR** 92/many sites sampled. **OR** Large sample size/number of repeats.	1	
		(ii)	Only 1 site showed latrines. **OR** No independent replicate.	1	
	(d)		• Latrines may have been washed away. • Some sites not surveyed due to deep water. • 5km between sample sites may miss vole territories. • No evidence that decrease due to predation/mink. **OR** No data for mink population. **OR** Other predators of vole may exist. **(Any two)**	2	
6.	(a)		Presence of (Sry) gene on the Y chromosome.	1	
	(b)		Temperature of (egg) incubation. **OR** Idea: ratio of males to females will alter at different temperatures.	1	
	(c)	(i)	Males lack homologous alleles on Y chromosome (so recessive allele always expressed). **OR** Males have one X so recessive allele always expressed. **OR** Males only need one (copy of) recessive allele (to be affected by the disease).	1	
		(ii)	X- (chromosome) inactivation is **random**. (1) Half the (kidney) cells will have a functional copy of the (ADH) receptor/gene. (1)	2	**Accept:** working = non-mutated = functional
		(iii)	50 (%)	1	

Question			Expected answer(s)	Max mark	Additional guidance
7.	(a)		Ethogram	1	
	(b)		(Use start times to) calculate duration of each behaviour to calculate proportion of time spent doing each behaviour.	1	
	(c)		Applying human activity/emotions/ traits to humans so behaviour misinterpreted/ conclusions not valid.	1	**Accept:** • human activity = perceptions = motivations = inferences
	(d)		Remote recording. **OR** Example such as • use cameras • use camera traps • video footage • satellite.	1	
8.			1. **Parasite** benefits at expense of **host.** 2. Example of parasite. 3. Parasite and host interact closely/frequently. **OR** Parasite and host **co-evolve**. 4. (In co-evolution) change in the traits of one species acts as a selection pressure on the other species. **OR** Idea of evolutionary arms race. 5. (RQ hypothesis states species must) adapt/evolve/ change to survive/avoid extinction. 6. Hosts that are better able to resist/tolerate parasites/have greater fitness/survival/number of offspring. **OR** Parasites that are better able to feed/reproduce/ find new hosts/have greater fitness/survival/ number of offspring. 7. Sexual reproduction generates (genetic) variation. 8. (Variation) provides raw material for adaptation/ evolution/natural selection. **(Any five)**	5	**Pt 2:** • To include bacteria/viruses/ protists/ platyhelminths/ nematodes/ fungi/arthropods • Named e.g.s acceptable • Flat/round worms acceptable.
9.	(a)		Trait disappears in group treated (with antibiotic then hypothesis is supported). **(1)** Compared to a control/no treatment/no antibiotic group (where no males produced). **(1)**	2	**Note:** • Trait = all female offspring. • Trait disappears = idea of males being produced again/sex ratio restored.
	(b)		Transfer of genetic material (from one bacterium to another) outwith reproduction/within same generation.	1	

Question			Expected answer(s)	Max mark	Additional guidance
	(c)		Purpose – to attract males (for breeding). (1) Females are competing so only occurs when males are in short supply. (1)	2	
	(d)		Protect/care for/carry young OR feed young OR build nest. **OR** (Greater) parental care.	1	Eggs = offspring = young. **NOT:** • Answers exemplified by *Acraea*. • Just parental investment.
10.	(a)		Epidemiology/epidemiological.	1	
	(b)		(Epidemics/outbreaks/measles) occurring (roughly) every 2 years.	1	**Accept:** Up one year and down the next
	(c)		As vaccination (uptake) increases, cases decrease.	1	
	(d)	(i)	Articles evaluated by experts **in the field.**	1	**Accept:** Academic = scientist = expert
		(ii)	With larger number of susceptible individuals. **OR** Number of immune individuals falls below the herd immunity threshold. **AND** Infection more easily transferred/spread/transmitted.	1	
		(iii)	(In Swansea) as vaccinations go down number of cases increases.	1	
	(e)		Herd immunity.	1	

11.	A	(i)	1. Tertiary structure is a folded polypeptide/3D shape.
			2. Shape/structure/conformation/folding determined by
			  One from:
			  • order of amino acids/R groups
			  • R-group interactions
			  • primary structure.
			3. **Two** R-groups named from:
			  • basic/positively charged
			  • acidic/negatively charged
			  • polar
			  • hydrophobic/non-polar.
			4. Named types of interactions.
			  One from:
			  • ionic bonds
			  • hydrogen bonds
			  • van der Waals interactions (London dispersion forces)
			  • disulphide bridges
			  • hydrophobic interactions.
			5. One other named from Pt 4.
			                   (Any three)
				9	Protein = polypeptide

Question			Expected answer(s)	Max mark	Additional guidance
		(ii)	a. Hydrophilic/polar (R) groups (mostly) at the surface of a soluble protein.		**Pt d.** Accept labelled diagram **Pt e.** Intrinsic = integral Extrinsic = peripheral
			b. (Soluble protein) found in the cytoplasm.		
			c. (In soluble proteins) hydrophobic groups may cluster at the centre (of protein).		
			d. Correct reference to membrane structure (with hydrophilic and hydrophobic regions).		
			e. Membrane proteins are integral or peripheral (both terms needed).		
			f. (Some integral proteins are) transmembrane + one example from: • channels • transporters • receptors.		
			g. W.r.t. integral proteins: idea of hydrophobic R groups interacting with hydrophobic region of membrane. **OR** Hydrophilic R groups interact with cytoplasm/extracellular environment.		
			h. Peripheral proteins have fewer hydrophobic R groups interacting with the phospholipids. **OR** Peripheral proteins have hydrophilic R groups interacting with hydrophilic heads of phospholipids/membrane proteins. **(Any six)**		
	B	(i)	1. Membrane has hydrophilic and hydrophobic regions.	9	
			2. Polar/charged/hydrophilic substances can't cross/pass through (membrane). **OR** Hydrophobic/non polar substances can cross/pass through (membrane).		
			3. Oxygen/carbon dioxide/water pass through.		
			4. Protein channels/pumps/transporters needed for hydrophilic/polar/charged substances to cross. **(Any two)**		

Question			Expected answer(s)	Max mark	Additional guidance
		(ii)	a. Channels/pumps/transporters are transmembrane.	7	
			b. Control ion concentrations **OR** Create/maintain concentration gradients.		
			c. Different cell types/cell compartments have different channel/transporter proteins **OR** example.		
			d. Movement through channels is passive/by diffusion/down a concentration gradient.		
			e. Transporter proteins change conformation (to transport molecules across membrane).		
			f. Conformational change in **active transport** requires energy from (hydrolysis of) ATP.		
			g. Ligand-gated channels opened/closed **by binding of signal molecules/ligand.**		
			h. Voltage-gated channels opened/closed **by changes in ion concentration.**		
			i. **One from:** **Na/KATPase** • Maintains osmotic balance in animal cells • Generates ion gradient for glucose symport • Generates and maintains resting potentials in neurons • Generates ion gradient in kidney tubules. **OR** **Aquaporin 2/AQP2** • Transports water in the collecting duct. **OR** GLUT4 Transports glucose in fat/muscle cells.		
			j. Second example from i.		
			(Any seven)		

Acknowledgements

Permission has been sought from all relevant copyright holders and Hodder Gibson is grateful for the use of the following:

Image © Artush/Shutterstock.com (SQP Section 2 page 19);
Image © petarg/Shutterstock.com (2016 Section 2 page 12);
Two images © Bildagentur Zoonar GmbH/Shutterstock.com (2016 Section 2 page 22);
Image © Ian Schofield/Shutterstock.com (2017 Section 2 page 14);
Image © Stephan Morris/Shutterstock.com (2017 Section 2 page 14);
Image © Eric Isselee/Shutterstock.com (2017 Section 2 page 18);
A quote from 'Life Ascending – The Ten Great Inventions of Evolution' by Nick Lane, published by Profile Books Ltd © Nick Lane, 2009, 2010 (2017 Section 2 page 20).